Critical praise for
Spalding Gray and *Swimming to Cambodia*

"The image that will stay with most of us is a picture of Mr. Gray talking and talking, anchored by a plain table, with a sheaf of notes at hand. It's conventional to think of Mr. Gray as relentlessly autobiographical. And yet the real autobiography in his monologues wasn't what he said so much as the way he connected what he was saying. Profound suffering was only an ellipsis away from comic anxiety."

New York Times

"Spalding is breaking new ground . . . he has accomplished the most difficult task for a writer—to speak for himself with no frills and no pretense."

Sam Shepard

"Gray fishes up much of the glory and chaos of our time . . . Talking about himself—with candor, humor, imagination and the unfailingly bizarre image—he ends up talking about all of us."

Washington Post

"His art is almost closer to that of a magician. Gray draws a graceful, sometimes invisible line from the primal to the avant-garde."

Los Angeles Herald Examiner

"Gray is more than a consummate storyteller. He is a passionate tour guide, probing the tortured labyrinth of the American psyche . . . an unholy cross between James Joyce and Hunter S. Thompson."

Sydney Morning Herald

SWIMMING TO CAMBODIA

SWIMMING TO CAMBODIA

Spalding Gray

THEATRE COMMUNICATIONS GROUP

Acknowledgments

Poem extract on page 71 from "Of Mere Being," in *The Palm at the End of the Mind* by Wallace Stevens, copyright © 1967, 1969, 1971 by Holly Stevens; New York: Alfred A. Knopf, Inc.; used by permission of the publisher. Quotations on page 125 from *The Cocktail Party* by T. S. Eliot, copyright © 1950, 1978 by Esme Valerie Eliot; New York: Harcourt Brace Jovanovich (U.S.) and Faber and Faber (Great Britain); used by permission of the publishers. Lines on page 44 from "Killing Me Softly with His Song" used by permission of Charles Fox and Norman Gimbel, copyright © 1972 by Charles Fox and Norman Gimbel. All rights reserved.

This publication is made possible in part with public funds from the New York State Council on the Arts, a State Agency.

TCG books are exclusively distributed to the book trade by Consortium Book Sales and Distribution, 1045 Westgate Drive, St. Paul, MN 55114.

Library of Congress Cataloging-in-Publication Data

Gray, Spalding, 1941–2004
Swimming to Cambodia.
1. Gray, Spalding, 1941–2004 —Journeys—Cambodia. 2. Cambodia—Description and travel—1975– 3. Moving-picture actors and actresses—United States—Biography. 4. Killing fields.
ISBN-13: 978-1-55936-254-2
ISBN-10: 1-55936-254-5
I. Title.
PN2287.G6759A37   1985   791.43'028'0924   [B]   85–20875

Cover and frontis photographs by Paula Court
Cover design by John Gall
Text design by Joe Marc Freedman

New Edition, February 2005

To the Cambodians and Cambodia,
a country beyond my imagination and
much too far to swim to.

Contents

▽   ▽   ▽   ▽   ▽   ▽

About the Author

▽　　▽　　▽　　▽　　▽　　▽

Roger Rosenblatt

He said that you can't be present in the place you're in until you've left, and want to go back. He also said that his two favorite Dollies were Parton and Lama. Spalding the mystical. Spalding the hilarious. Spalding the self-exposed, the professionally puzzled, the scared, the brave. Spalding the supporting actor. That's what he was in the movies. But as a writer and a stage performer, he changed the idea of what a supporting actor is. He supported us. He played our part—we who wish to think that we're the stars of the show, but who, in our shaky, collapsible hearts know better, and yet who know, too, that we have a significance somewhere.

Spalding the storyteller. We constitute a narrative species, we humans. We like to tell one another that we're a rational species, but given human behavior in places such as Cambodia, that idea has become more of a bitter joke. A narrative species is something else, and closer to the mark. We learn by stories, live by stories, evolve by telling the story of ourselves in the half-vain, half-beautiful hope that one day we may get our story right.

In the process, we tacitly elect a few to be the chief tellers of our tales. Spalding was one of the elected. The specialty of his storytelling was the search for a sorrow that could be alchemized into a myth. He went for the misery sufficiently deep to create a story that makes us laugh.

So doing, he invented a form, a very rare thing among artists. Some called it the "epic monologue" because first it was spoken and then it was written, like the old epics, and because it consisted of great and important themes drawn from the hero's life. But as an epic hero, Spalding told his stories standing on his head. Instead of exhibiting a single tragic flaw, he was all flaws. (Spalding would have said that he crawled around on all flaws.) And the one true heroic element in his makeup was the willingness to be open, rapidly open, about his confusions, his frailties.

At the same time, he understood that openness was his protection. The monologue kept him safe from others, just as did the table (his set) at which he sat. The monologue protected him from dialogue. And it also allowed him to be open, rapidly open, to images. The thing about good writing is that it never starts with an idea. It is the image, always the image, that comes first, arising in the murky fluid of the writer's mind like the answers in a Magic 8 Ball. Without explanation and bearing no map, it simply appears and it beckons. The writer follows.

On a day off from shooting *The Killing Fields*, Spalding finds himself chatting among correspondents, whom he calls Real People, as distinct from actors, and still he occupies his own sphere: "And then there was me, who was looking at this incredible bee that looked like the cartoon of a bee because it was so big and fluffy, and its stripes were so wide, and I was saying, 'Wow! Look at these bees.' And everyone said, 'It's just a bee, Spalding.'"

No one ever was better at the art of digression. Spalding digressed from life. He digressed from the narrative. He made narratives out of his digressions from life. Holden Caulfield, a kindred threatened nomadic spirit, was in speech class where the students were coached to cry out: "Digression! Digression!" whenever a speaker wandered off the point—Salinger's own point being that only by wandering does one get anywhere. For Spalding, "Where was I?" was not a rhetorical device; it was both a profound and funny question. Throughout *Swimming to Cambodia* he thrives on getting lost in the lost country, and only when we are lost with him, do we get somewhere.

Missed opportunities, missed appointments, missed dates; they are the substance of his art, all confessed in that unbuttered-toast voice of his, which was the perfect instrument of the funny serious man. He said, "I'm interested in creative confession. I would have made a great Catholic." Not to be parochial about it, but I think that he would have made a better Jew, free to be guilty as hell, yet without the safety net of ritual. Specifically, I think he would have made a great Oscar Levant, artistically in control of his chaos, for as long as he could be, and turning the noise in his head into music.

One time Spalding rattled himself by realizing that he actually had enjoyed a day. Then he followed that realization with this: "After all, think of all that could have gone wrong." Once he says that, of course, he is off to Spalding Land, and we know that we are in for a monstrous inventory of all that could have gone wrong that day: corrosive diseases; attacks from outer space, financial ruin, the usual, until we are certain—as he intended us to be—that it was a disastrous day after all. And instead of feeling content, we are hurled into an imagined depression. No one ever could be so sublimely miserable.

That sort of drifty flight (or nose dive) was a key to Spalding. He could dream into what he knew. He could imagine what already had happened. The casual power of *Swimming to Cambodia*—the memory of murder and catastrophe, the loveliness of the country mixed in with the desperate desire to swim *away* from Cambodia, and the basic sweetness of the soul who guides us—all depend on his ability to dream into the past. By his looking back, it seems as if he could rescue the past, rescue us from the past, and himself as well, up to a point. Spalding survived like a champ. He kept his head above water, up to a point, which is why the cover of the earlier edition of this book, with his face half-submerged, breaks our hearts.

His last adventure (perhaps next to last) occurred on a ferry boat that travels between two islands. He had something unknown on his mind. There was that other ferry boat in Greek mythology that traveled between the realms of the living and the dead. There was that quotation he liked from Eliot's *Four Quartets* about one forever exploring, then arriving where one started and seeing it for the first time. Whatever he was thinking on that sad day, it is certain that he made the world wiser, funnier, and more alert to its most useful sorrow. By attempting to swim to Cambodia, he discovered the misery sufficiently deep to create a story that makes us laugh: Spalding the story.

Author's Note

▽   ▽   ▽   ▽   ▽   ▽

In *Conversations with Jorge Luis Borges* the author relates, "I remember my father said to me something about memory. He said, 'I thought I could recall my childhood when we first came to Buenos Aires, but now I know that I can't . . . . Every time I recall something I'm not recalling it really, I'm recalling the last time I recalled it, I'm recalling my last memory of it.' "

Swimming to Cambodia evolved over two years and almost two hundred performances. It was constructed by recalling the first image in my memory of each previous performance, so it evolved almost like a children's "Round Robin" game in which a phrase is whispered around and around a circle until the new phrase is stated aloud and compared with the original. The finished product is a result of a series of organic, creative mistakes—perception itself becoming the editor of the final report.

It is this subconscious way of working, rather than any conscious contrivance or manipulation, that captures my imagination. I am interested in what happens to the so-called facts after they have passed through performance and registered on my memory. Each performance becomes like another person whispering a slightly altered phrase. My job is then to let my intuitive side make choices—and there is never a lack of material, because all human culture is art. It is all a conscious contrivance for the purpose of survival. All I have to do is look at what's around me.

So I like to think of myself as a kind of "poetic reporter," more like an impressionist painter than a photographer. Most reporters get the facts out as quickly as possible—fresh news is the best news. I do just the opposite. I give the facts a chance to settle down until at last they blend, bubble and mix in the swamp of dream, memory and reflection.

It was almost six months after the filming of *The Killing Fields* that I began my first reports, and more than two years passed before I made my last adjustments. Over that time, *Swimming to Cambodia* evolved into a very personal work in which I made the experience my own. Life made a theme of itself and finally transformed itself into a work of fiction.

I titled this work *Swimming to Cambodia* when I realized that to try to imagine what went on in that country during the gruesome period from 1966 to the present would be a task equal to swimming there from New York. Still, in spite of how horrible it seems to allow entire nations to be wiped out, I opted for tolerance, and beneath tolerance, my bottom line, humor. If ever I thought that God could understand American, I would pray and the prayer would go, "Dear God, please, please let us keep our sense of humor." I still understand and love America, precisely for its sense of humor.

When, in Woody Allen's film *Stardust Memories*, a group of extra-terrestrials lands in his proximity, Woody hopes to get some answers. He asks, "Shouldn't I stop making movies and do something that counts, like helping blind people or becoming a missionary or something?" The otherworldly reply: "You want to do mankind a *real* service? Tell funnier jokes." Humor. The bottom line.

I'm convinced that all meaning is to be found only in reflection. *Swimming to Cambodia* is an attempt at that kind of reflection.

I would like to thank Peter Wollen for telling Susie Figgis to look me up when she came to New York, and Bob Carrol for giving Susie my phone number once she arrived. My thanks, also, to Roland Joffe, a fine director, and David Puttnam, a courageous producer, for giving me the opportunity to be a part of the incredible experience that became *The Killing Fields*; to the more than 150 people who were part of that project; and especially to those either directly mentioned by name or referred to in *Swimming to Cambodia*—my appreciation for their indulgence and willingness to be included in this most unlikely by-product of the film. I would also like to give credit and thanks to William Shawcross for his tremendously informative book *Sideshow* (Simon & Schuster, 1979), from which I drew much of my historic material. I am also indebted to Sidney Schanberg and Elizabeth Becker for their personal contributions. I am deeply grateful to Elizabeth LeCompte and all the members of The Wooster Group for their faithful and fruitful occupation of The Performing Garage, the nurturing center from which this work has grown; and Richard Schechner, who first opened that garage door to let me in off the streets.

Thanks, too, to Renée Shafransky for her loving support. Finally, many thanks to TCG publications director Terry Nemeth and Laura Ross, my editor, who had the vision to see what they first heard as a written piece; and Jim Leverett, for his faithful and articulate coverage of my work over the years.

—S.G.
August 1985

SWIMMING TO CAMBODIA

part one

It was the first day off in a long time, and all of us were trying to get a little rest and relaxation out by the pool at this big, modern hotel that looked something like a prison. If I had to call it anything I would call it a "pleasure prison." It was the kind of place you might come to on a package tour out of Bangkok. You'd come down on a chartered bus— and you'd probably not wander off the grounds because of the high barbed-wire fence they have to keep you in and the bandits out. And every so often you would hear shotguns going off as the hotel guards fired at rabid dogs down along the beach on the Gulf of Siam.

But if you really wanted to walk on the beach, all you had to learn to do was to pick up a piece of seaweed, shake it in the dog's face and everything would be hunky-dory.

So it was our first day off in a long time and there were about 130 of us out by the pool trying to get a little rest and relaxation, and the Thai waiters were running and jumping over hedges to bring us "Kloster! More Kloster!" Everyone was ordering Kloster beer. No one was ordering the Singah because someone had said that Singah, which is exported to the United States, has formaldehyde in it. The waiters were running and jumping over hedges because they couldn't get to us fast enough. They were running and jumping and smiling—not a silly smile but a profound smile, a deep smile. There was nothing idiotic about it because the Thais have a word, *sanug*, which, loosely translated, means "fun." And they never do anything that isn't *sanug*—if it isn't *sanug* they won't touch it.

Some say that the Thais are the nicest people that money can buy, because they like to have fun. They know how to have fun and, perhaps due to their very permissive strain of Buddhism, they don't have to suffer for it after they have it.

It was a lovely day and we were all out by the pool and the Sparks—the British electricians were called "the Sparks"—were out there with their Thai wives. They had had the good sense—or bad sense, depending on how you look at it—as soon as they arrived in Bangkok, to go down to Pat Pong and buy up women to travel with them. I was told that each man bought two women so as not to risk falling in love. And there the Sparks were, lying like 250-pound beached whales while their ninety-pound "Thai wives," in little two-piece bathing suits, walked up and down on them giving them Shiatsu massages as a Thai waiter ran, jumped over the hedge, tripped and fell, hurling his Klosters down to explode on the cement by the pool. And looking up with a great smile he said, "Sorry sir, we just run out of Kloster."

Ivan (Devil in My Ear), a South African and head of the second camera unit—and a bit of a Mephisophelian figure—said, "Spalding, there's a party tonight up on the Gulf of Siam. Could I come over and borrow your toenail clippers?"

"Sure."

"Shall I bring some Thai stick? Do you want to smoke a joint before we go?"

I thought, why not? It's a day off and I haven't smoked since I've been here. Why not give it a try?

Now, every time I've been in a country where the marijuana is supposed to be really good—Mexico, India, Northern California and now Thailand—I've always felt that I should try it. Maybe this time it would be different. Maybe this time I would be able to sleep, like so many people say they do. Maybe this time I'd have a sense of well-being and feel at one with the world. You see, marijuana tends to unlock my Kundalini in the worst way and all the energy just gets stuck in my lower Chakra. It just gets stuck and spins there like a snake chasing its tail, or a Studebaker stuck in sand.

So I said, "Sure, bring it over."

Then I thought, maybe I should have waited until I'd spoken with Renée first. Renée was over there visiting me for fourteen days and we planned to go back to New York together as soon as I finished the film. We had rented a summer house together in upstate New York, in Krummville, and Krummville was looking less and less exotic to me the longer I stayed in Thailand. You see, I hadn't had a Perfect Moment yet, and I always like to have one before I leave an exotic place. They're a good way of bringing things to an end. But you can never plan for one. You never know when they're coming. It's sort of like falling in love . . . with yourself.

Also, I was beginning to get this image of myself as a kind of wandering poet-bachelor-mendicant beating my way down the whole coast of Malaysia, eating magic mushrooms all the way, until I finally reach Bali and evaporate into the sunset in a state of ecstasy. But I wasn't telling Renée that. I was only telling her that I wasn't sure when I would be coming back, and that was enough to enrage her. We fell into a big fight on the way to the party that lasted all the way down to the Gulf of Siam. And there we were, arguing on this fantastic beach where, unlike the Hamptons, there was no boat and a bigger boat, no ship and a bigger ship, no carrot and the carrot and desire and desire. It was just one big beach with no boats. Nothing to buy. Just one big piece of calendar art.

And Renée and I were walking down the beach arguing and I said, "Stop, Renée. Stop with the fighting. Look at this beautiful sunset. Look! Look! I might be able to have a Perfect Moment right now and we could go home."

But Renée would have none of it. She's very confrontational and always wants to talk about what is going on in the relationship, not the sunset. So she went off to cry on Therese's shoulder and talk to Julian, and I went to Ivan (Devil in My Ear) who said, "Spalding, don't let her get the upper hand, man. I mean, after all, how many straight, single men your age are there left in New York City anyway? What's she going to do?"

And I said, "Ivan, no, don't say things like that."

Then Renée and I came out of our respective corners and went back at it for another round, until at last she said, "Listen, I'll give you an ultimatum. Either you marry me or you give me a date when you're coming back."

I thought for a minute and said, "July 8. I'll be back on July 8."

Then it was time for the pleasure. We had fought and made up and it was time for the *sanug*. That's the order in which we do it in our culture. So we went down to the beach with Ivan and sat at the water's edge. By then it was dark and gentle waves were lapping as party sounds drifted in the distance. We were the only ones down on the beach, under the stars, and it was almost too much, too beautiful to bear. Ivan lit the Thai stick and passed it down.

I took three deep tokes and as I held the smoke in, this overwhelming wave of anxiety came over me. I closed my eyes and saw this pile of black and brown shit steaming on the edge of a stainless steel counter. The shit was cold and yet it was steaming, and I somehow knew that it represented all of the negative energy in my mind. I could see a string extending from between my eyes to the shit and I knew that if I pulled that string with my head I could pull all that shit right off the edge of that stainless steel counter. I started to pull and as I was pulling I could see that next to the shit was this pile of bubbly pastel energy floating about two inches off the stainless steel counter. I saw that this pastel energy was connected to the shit through these tendrils that ranged from pastel to shit-brown. It was then I realized that if I pulled the negative energy off the counter I would pull the positive off with it, and I'd be left with nothing but a stainless steel counter, which I was not yet ready for in my life. And at the moment I realized that, the counter turned into a tunnel I was going down at the speed of the Santa Cruz roller coaster. But the tunnel was not black this time so I knew I was getting healthier. It was gold-leaf, and the leaves were spreading like palm leaves or like the iris of a big eye as I picked up speed and headed for the center of the Earth, until I was going so fast that I couldn't stand it anymore and I pulled back, opened my eyes, grabbed the beach and let out a great WHOOOA. . . .

When I opened my eyes Ivan was there but Renée was gone. She must have wandered off down the beach. I had no real sense of where I was. It all looked and felt like a demented Wallace Stevens poem with food poisoning, and in the distance I saw what looked like a group of Thai girl scouts dancing around a campfire. I thought that if I could get in that circle and hold hands with them I would be whole again. I would be cured and back in real time. I got up and tried to walk toward the fire and found that I was falling down like a Bowery bum, like a drunken teenager or the fraternity brother I'd never been. And all of a sudden I realized I was going to be very sick and I crawled off like a Thai dog to a far corner of the beach.

Up it came, and each time the vomit hit the ground I covered it over with sand, and the sand I covered it with turned into a black gauze death mask that flew up and covered my face. And so it went; vomit-cover-mask, vomit-cover-mask, until I looked down to see that I had built an entire corpse in the sand and it was my corpse. It was my own decomposing corpse staring back at me, and I could see the teeth pushing through the rotting lips and the ribs coming through the decomposing flesh of my side. I looked up to see Renée standing over me saying, "What's wrong, Hon?"

"I'm dying, that's what's wrong."

"Oh. I thought you were having a good time building sand castles."

She had been looking on at a distance.

Two men, I don't know who, carried me out of there, one arm over one shoulder and one arm over another, like a drunken, crucified sailor. And I was very upset because the following day I was scheduled to do my big scene in the movie.

In February of '83 I met this incredible British documentary filmmaker, Roland Joffe. He was very in tense—a combination of Zorro, Jesus and Rasputin— body of Zorro, heart of Jesus and eyes of Rasputin. Roland had come to New York to cast a new film called *The Killing Fields*, produced by David Puttnam, and I was called in for an audition. Peter Wollen had seen one of my monologues and told Susie Figgis, who was helping cast the film, about me and she had set up an audition with Roland.

It was unlike any audition I'd ever been to before. Roland didn't have me read; he didn't even ask me any questions. He did all of the talking while I listened, and he talked and talked. He talked for about forty minutes nonstop. Roland told me the story of *The Killing Fields*.

It was the story of a *New York Times* reporter named Sidney Schanberg and his sidekick, Dith Pran, who was a Cambodian photographer. It was about how they covered and reported the story of the Americans' secret bombing of Cambodia, and how Schanberg and Pran stayed behind in Phnom Penh after the American embassy was evacuated because they wanted to cover what happened when the Khmer Rouge marched in. They wanted to find out if there was going to be a "bloodbath" or not, so they fled to the French embassy to hide out, and when the Khmer Rouge marched into the city they went directly to the French embassy and demanded, "All Cambodians out or everyone dies." So Dith Pran had to be expelled to almost certain death because the Khmer Rouge were killing any Cambodian who was connected with Americans. Pran was given up for dead by most, but Schanberg never gave up hope and kept searching until, after three years, he located Pran in a Thai refugee camp. He brought him to New York City where Pran now works for *The New York Times*.

"Great story," I said. "Sounds fantastic. Sounds like someone made it up. I want to tell you that I would love to play any role in this film, just to be in it. But I must also confess that I know nothing about what you've told me. I'm not very political—in fact, I've never even voted in my life."

And Roland said, "Perfect! We're looking for the American ambassador's aide."

He went on, "But I'm not saying you have the role. I have a lot of other people to see and I have to see how it all shapes up and fits together with casting. I'm going out to the Coast to see some people and I'll be back in a couple of months. Let's chat again then."

I said goodbye and left, and as I went out of the room I thought, I really want to be in that film. In fact, I want to be in that film more than any project I've ever been approached for. At the same time, I had no idea what I could actively do to get the role. That was a large part of why I had stopped trying to be a professional actor in the first place; I couldn't stand all the waiting while that big, indifferent machine made up its so-called mind. I wanted some power and influence over the events of my life.

I couldn't stand leaving it all to chance, and the first idea that occurred to me was *prayer*. But I thought, it's been so long, God would know I was in bad faith.

The next thing that occurred to me was *contacts*. Well, no, maybe *contacts* was first and *prayer* was second. . . . But anyway, I didn't have any contacts within the British film industry. So the next voice that came to me was that old logical, coping voice we all know so well: "Well, if I get it, I get it. If I don't, I don't. I'll do something else. After all, I can still *see* and *walk*." And my mother had always said, "Think of the starving Koreans." I was trying to do that.

But my illogical, preconscious voice would have none of this, and set up a condition I would have to call Compulsive Magical Thinking, which soon got quite out of control.

It all started innocently enough in my living loft. I found that I was unable to leave my loft without turning my little KLH radio off on a positive word. And do you know how difficult those words are to find these days? I would just stand there by the radio with my hand on the little knob so I could turn it off real fast when I heard the positive word.

"The stock market is *rising.*" (click)

". . . consider moving Marines to *safer . . .*" (click)

"You may go to a doctor that belongs to the AMA but it doesn't necessarily mean you're going to the *best.*" (click)

And then I could leave my loft. And as I went out I found that I would turn the doorknob three times. Threes became very important, as did right shoe in front of left shoe. I always made sure that I put my right shoe ahead of my left shoe when I left them by the bed. I led with my right foot as I started up the street, snapping my fingers three times, then in sets of three, then three fingers in sets of six, as I walked up to the supermarket to buy soup, where every third can was fine. The first two had botulism.

Then I went on to Barnes & Noble, snapping all the way, in search of books on Cambodia. When I got there I went to the piles of books in the Annex and, pulling out every third book, I whispered to myself, "Now this has power."

Then I turned and saw a man behind me fleeing from stack to stack. I knew he didn't work for Barnes & Noble because of his overcoat and the wads of newspaper stuck in his ears and I thought, this is one of the therapeutic joys of living in New York City. It always works. As soon as you think you're crazy, all you have to do is look over your shoulder.

It wasn't long before these little compulsions got more elaborate and the condition more complex. I was walking down the street and I saw a man coming toward me and I thought, I've got to keep this lamppost on my right and the man on my left and have us all line up perpendicular just at the end of the third snap in a series of six finger snaps. Then I thought, wait a minute, lamppost on right or man on right? Which is more important, man or lamppost? And, wham. I ran into the man.

It was then that I realized it was getting out of hand. I thought, I'd better slow down with this stuff or I'll get put away before I even get the role in the movie. I guess it was then that the "Little King" took over. The superego figure took charge and set up an alternative condition that was very new for me. I'd have to call it a Will. And the Little King superego figure proclaimed that if I willed my Will to stop this Magical Thinking then this act of will, willing Will, would have more power toward getting me the role in the film.

Around the time I was developing my Will I was invited out to Los Angeles to perform my monologues. I got good reviews so Warner Brothers Television called me up and said, "Could you come in and read? Anything, just come in and read."

"Come up and see my monologue, why don't you? It's just up the street."

"Well, we haven't got time for that, we go to bed early out here. But could you come in?"

And what they chose for me to read was a sitcom— a pilot that had been "axed" or "cut" or whatever the technical term is for a show that's been put on the shelf because it's no good. So that was the text.

I was to be reading the role of Howard and my wife was Harriet. I started out, "But I don't want to spend my Sundays eating mixed nuts in the company of your sister and her jerky husband."

Harriet answered, "Oh come on. You know you really like Norman."

"Harriet, the idea of Norman doesn't put a smile on any part of my body."

"Get ready. Put your shoes on."

"Why? They know I have feet."

"Come on, you know it's become a tradition to have them over on Sundays."

"Tradition? Now listen Harriet. Decorating a Christmas tree is a tradition. Fireworks on the Fourth is a tradition. But having your sister and her jerky husband over here to park their carcasses on my couch, watch my TV and scarf down all the cashews from the mixed-nut bowl is not my idea of a tradition!"

I didn't get the role. I think I read it with too much of an edge, actually. Too East Coast intellectual. So I was on my way out and—the Lord works in strange ways—lo and behold, I ran into Roland Joffe, who was there casting *The Killing Fields*. Warner Brothers was putting money into the film and they were going to distribute it, so they were letting him use an office. Roland said, "Let's chat again."

I went home and put on my white shirt and my pink tie and my tweed jacket and went back to the studio. Once again Roland talked to me, this time for forty-five minutes. He did all the talking again, about what an incredible country Cambodia was before it was colonized, that it had a strain of Buddhism so permissive and so sensual that the Cambodians seemed to have done away with unnecessary guilt. Compared to Cambodia, Thailand was a Nordic country—Thailand was like Sweden compared to Cambodia, which was more like Italy. Ninety percent of the Cambodians owned their land—it was dirty land, it was earth, but it was clean. Earth dirt. Clean dirt. And they were so happy.

The Cambodians knew how to have fun. They knew how to have a good time being born; how to have a good time growing up; a good time going through puberty; a good time falling in love and staying in love; a good time getting married and having children; a good time raising children; and a good time growing old and dying. They even knew how to have a good time on New Year's Eve. I couldn't believe it.

The only thing, according to Roland, was that they had lost touch with evil. Because it was such a beautiful, gentle land, they'd lost touch with evil. The situation was something like that of the Tantric colonies on the East Coast of India. They were so open down there that the Huns just came in and ate them up like chocolate-covered cherries. And the same thing was happening to the Cambodians.

The Samoans, on the other hand, have a very pleasurable culture but they've made sure to initiate their children into pain through certain tattoo rituals, so that they have a realistic association with pain.

I couldn't get a clear vision of Cambodia in my mind. I had a map in my head, but I couldn't quite place it among the other countries—so I looked at a map and there it was, about the size of the state of Missouri. In 1965 there were about seven million people in the entire country, six hundred thousand in the capital of Phnom Penh. There's a big freshwater lake right in the middle for all sorts of recreational activities, fishing along the coast, seaports along the Gulf of Siam. And in 1966 that happy, sexy Prince Sihanouk—perhaps because of his Buddhist tolerance and open-mindedness—allowed the Vietnamese a few "sanctuaries" along the border.

The American Air Force got very upset about this, one general in particular, who was sure that there was a Central Headquarters up there about the size of the Pentagon from which the Vietnamese sent out orders. Maybe it was even a replica of the Pentgon—I think the Air Force thought that.

And if they could just bump off that Central Headquarters by flying in a few B-52s from Bangkok . . . they wouldn't even have to tell the American public about it. "Who needs to know about it? We can do it in one raid and we'd be done with that Central Headquarters." So the general called a secret meeting at the Pentagon, named, of course, Operation Breakfast. At Operation Breakfast they came up with *the menu*.

It was kind of a weird diet, as you can imagine. The bombers came up from Bangkok like big flying motels, dropping their bombs according to some computer program on all the sanctuaries, then up to where they thought the headquarters might be and all along the Ho Chi Minh supply line.

But instead of driving the Vietcong back, Operation Breakfast had the opposite effect. It drove them further into the Cambodian jungles where they hitched up with this weird bunch of rednecks called the Khmer Rouge, run by Pol Pot along with Khieu Samphan and Ieng Sary. They had been educated in Paris in the strict Maoist doctrine, except someone threw a perverse little bit of Rousseau into the soup.

This made for a strange bunch of bandits, hanging out in the jungle living on bark, bugs, leaves and lizards, being trained by the Vietcong. They had a back-to-the-land, racist consciousness beyond anything Hitler had ever dreamed of. But they had no scapegoat other than the city-dwellers of Phnom Penh. They were like a hundred thousand rednecks rallying in New Paltz, New York, ninety miles above the City, about to march in.

Now, around the time that the VC were up there training the Khmer Rouge, Sihanouk—who was out of town for a day—was deposed, maybe by a CIA plot. No one really knows about that. And Lon Nol was put in his place, General Lon Nol, formerly Prince Sihanouk's prime minister. No one knew anything about Lon Nol in the United States. As one political cartoonist noted at the time, the only thing we knew was that "Lon Nol" spelled backwards was "Lon Nol."

Well, leave it to a Brit to tell you your own history; the next thing that Roland told me was that, at that time, President Nixon was developing this madman theory on the banks of Key Biscayne. He said to Bob Haldeman, "Listen Bob, just let it be known that I've gone mad, see, and then the Vietcong will think that I'm going to press the button—you know how trigger-happy I am—and they'll stop all of their bombing."

In order to develop this madman theory he was

watching reruns of *Patton* in his bedroom every night, over and over again, and taking military advice from Bebe Rebozo and John Mitchell.

The incident at Kent State happened around then as well, as Roland reminded me. He suggested I read up on it in a book called *Sideshow*, by William Shawcross, which I did, later. I remembered Kent State but I had just lumped it in with the Vietnam protest; I'd forgotten that it was a direct protest against the invasion of Cambodia. I also didn't know that most U.S. National Guard troops were not allowed to have live ammunition in their guns, but in Ohio they were. Governor James Rhodes had called them out because the protesters were storming Kent's ROTC building, and on a lovely May day fifteen people were shot, four innocent bystanders were killed. Roland told me that the American public was polled on its reaction to the incident and the majority of people said that the shooting was justified. This caused enormous dissension and one hundred thousand protesters marched on the White House. Haig massed troops in the basement of the White House thinking there was going to be a siege. According to Shawcross, Nixon got no sleep at all; he was up the entire night making phone calls. He made fifty calls, eight to Kissinger, seven to Haldeman, one to Norman Vincent Peale, one to Billy Graham. After one hour of sleep he got up and put on Rachmaninoff's Concerto No. 1 and, with his Cuban valet Manolo Sanchez, he went down to the Lincoln Memorial to talk to the protesters about surfing, football, how travel broadens the mind. In fact, Roland reports that one of the students said, "I hope it was because our President was tired, but when he asked me what college I was from and I told him, he said, "How's your team doing this year?"

Now colleagues and friends—actually, I don't know if he had any *friends*—but colleagues of Kissinger wanted him to resign. And Kissinger said, "What if I resign and then the President has a heart attack? We'll be left with Agnew. That's the only reason I'm staying on. For national security."

Because of all this, the Cooper-Church Amendment went through. This was an amendment meant to stop any ground support troops from going into a country where war had not officially been declared by the Senate or Congress. But, as Roland reminded me, we're not living in a democracy. I had forgotten all about this: the President is the Commander-in-Chief of the Army and can simply bypass Senate and Congress. Which is just what he did. Nixon kept saying, "Bomb, bomb, bomb," and the bombs kept falling.

The only thing that the protest accomplished was to frighten Nixon enough that he declared, "No more close ground support troops more than twenty-one miles over the border into Cambodia." How they controlled that, I don't know, whether the troops had odometers strapped to their legs or what. But twenty-one miles in they had to go right back out, or turn into pumpkins.

During this time they sent Alexander Haig over to speak to Lon Nol because Lon Nol had been told that the American troops weren't going to be in Cambodia anymore. Lon Nol, of course, saw in this the downfall of his country. It was very clear; the handwriting was on the wall. He turned to the window and wept.

And Haig went back and reported this to the American government, that Lon Nol had cried in front of him. The American government was so upset that they sent over an official psychiatrist to examine Lon Nol for crying in public. He came back and reported that Lon Nol was an unstructured, vague individual. Not only that, but that he made astrological, occultist and folkloric references in his addresses to the nation. Can you imagine? "My fellow Americans, I am not going out for the next two weeks because my moon is in Gemini."

This freaked the Americans out, so they compiled a whole report on Lon Nol in which they detailed his weird rituals. One was to cut the skin of the troops to let in the spirit of Buddha. Another was to create the illusion that there were more troops than actually existed. (I don't know how they were supposed to have done this—with scarecrows or what—but it caused enormous extortion of American funds.) The third ritual was called "transference of grass into troops." I'm not sure what this means; I assume they were sending marijuana to the front, but I don't know why they would refer to marijuana as "grass" in a government report. Fourth, they faced all statues of Buddha in toward Phnom Penh and away from China in order to revitalize the city. Number five, the Cambodians debated but never settled on. The question was whether they should copy the old Khmer warriors' magical markings from the uniforms in their museums onto the soldiers' outfits. The markings had been meant to stop slings and arrows in the old days, but no one was sure they would be powerful enough to stop bullets. It was still in debate.

While that was being argued, according to Roland,

the unsung hero, Donald Dawson, reared his ugly head. He was a Christian Scientist flying B-52 raids out of Bangkok, but he was home on leave. He was watching *West Side Story* on television but all he could see were bombs falling, people screaming, dying—he was hallucinating. When he got back to flying his missions he found out that a Cambodian wedding party had been wiped out by accident. He held his own wedding to be the most sacred event in his life and he refused to fly anymore, so he was court-martialed.

Dawson got together with three other flyers who refused to fly and, with the help of New York congresswoman Elizabeth Holtzman and the ACLU, they began building a case to be taken to the Supreme Court. The Supreme Court had never dealt with the illegality of this bombing that had been going on for years, but it just so happened that at that time they weren't in session. The ACLU got the case to Thurgood Marshall, who was sympathetic. They then had to get it to William Douglas, who was in Goose Prairie, Washington, in a cabin in the hills, with no telephone. There didn't seem to be any way to reach him. But Burt Neuborn of the ACLU flew out to Goose Prairie, hiked in to the cabin, presented the case and Douglas was sympathetic as well.

The Supreme Court was about to meet and vote on the bombing when Donald Dawson received Conscientious Objector status from the U.S. Air Force, so they never met, the whole five years the bombing went on, the Supreme Court never met about it. And the generals still note with pride that the bombing killed twenty-five percent of the enemy. That's sixteen thousand killed, they say. And there's a military rule: If you kill more than ten percent of the enemy you cause irreversible psychological damage.

So that five years of bombing—along with the traditional diet of lizards, bugs, bark and leaves, education in the Maoist doctrine including a touch of Rousseau, and other things that we will never know about in our lifetimes including, perhaps, an invisible cloud of evil that circles the world and lands at random in Germany, Cambodia, possibly Iran and Beirut, maybe even America—set the Khmer Rouge up to carry out the worst auto-homeo-genocide in modern history.

Whenever I travel, if I have the time, I go by train. Because I like to hang out in the lounge car. I hear such great stories there—fantastic! Perhaps it's because they think they'll never see me again. It's like a big, rolling confessional.

I was on my way to Chicago from New York City when this guy came up to me and said, "Hi, I'm Jim Bean. Mind if I sit down?"

"No, I'm Spalding Gray, have a seat. What's up Jim?"

"Oh, nothing much. I'm in the Navy."

"Really? Where are you stationed?"

"Guantanamo Bay."

"Where's that?"

"Cuba."

"Really? What's it like?"

"Oh, we don't get into Cuba, man. It's totally illegal. We go down to the Virgin Islands whenever we want R & R. We get free flights down there."

"What do you do there?"

"Get laid."

"Go to whores?"

"No. I never paid for sex in my life. I get picked up by couples. I like to swing, I mean, I'm into that, you know? Threesomes, triangles, pyramids—there's power in that."

And I could see how he would be picked up. He was cute enough—insidious, but still cute. The only kind of demented thing about him was that his ears hadn't grown. They were like those little pasta shells. It was as if his body had grown but his ears hadn't caught up yet.

So I said, "Where are you off to?"

"Pittsburgh."

"Pittsburgh, my god. What's up there?"

"My wife."

"Really? How long has it been since you saw her?"

"Oh, about a year."

"I bet she's been doing some swinging herself."

"No, man, I know her. She's got fucking cobwebs growing between her legs. I wouldn't mind watching her get fucked by a guy once, no, I wouldn't mind that at all."

"Well that's quite a trip, coming from Cuba to Pittsburgh."

"No, no. I'm not stationed in Cuba anymore, man. I'm in Philly."

"Oh, well what's going on in Philly?"

"Can't tell you. No way. Top secret."

"Oh, come on, Jim. Top secret in Philadelphia? You can tell me."

"No way."

And he proceeded to have five more rum cokes and tell me that in Philadelphia he is on a battleship in a waterproof chamber, chained one arm to the wall for five hours a day, next to a green button, with earphones on. I could just see those little ears waiting for orders to fire his rockets from their waterproof silos onto the Russians. He sits there waiting with those earphones on, high on blue-flake cocaine, a new breed from Peru that he loves, with a lot of coffee because the Navy can't test for cocaine. They can test for marijuana five days after you smoke a joint, but not the cocaine. He sits there high on cocaine, chained to the wall, next to the green button, in a waterproof chamber.

"Why waterproof?" I asked. I thought I'd just start with the details and work out. I know I could have said, "Why a green button?," but it didn't matter at that point.

"Waterproof, man, because when the ship sinks and I go down to the bottom of the ocean, any ocean, anywhere, I'm still there in my waterproof chamber and I can push that green button, activate my rocket and it fires out of the waterproof silo and up, up, up it goes. I get a fucking erection every time I think of firing a rocket on those Russians. We're going to win! We're going to win this fucking war. I like the Navy, though. I fucking *like* the Navy. I get to travel everywhere. I've been to Africa, Sweden, India. I fucking didn't like Africa, though. I don't know why, but black women just don't turn me on."

Now here's a guy, if the women in the country don't turn him on, he misses the entire landscape. It's just one big fuzzball, a big black outline and he steps through to the other side of the world and comes out in Sweden.

"I fucking love Sweden, man. You get to see real Russkies in Sweden. They're marched in at gunpoint and they're only allowed two beers. We're drinking all the fucking beer we want. We're drunk on our asses, saying, 'Hey, Russkies, what's it like in Moscow this time of year?' And then we pay a couple of Swedish whores to go over and put their heads in the Russkies' laps. You should see those fuckers sweat, man. They are so stupid. We're going to win. We're going to win the fuckin' war. I mean, they are really *dumb*. They've got liquid fuel in their rockets, they're rusty and they're going to sputter, they're going to pop, they're going to land in our cornfields."

"Wait a minute, Jim. Cornfields? I mean, haven't you read the literature? It's bad enough if they land in the cornfields. We're all doomed."

"No, they're stupid. You won't believe this. The Russians don't even have electro-intercoms in their ships. They still speak through tubes!"

Suddenly I had this enormous fondness for the Russian Navy. The whole of Mother Russia. The thought of these men speaking, like innocent children, through empty toilet paper rolls, where you could still hear compassion, doubt, envy, brotherly love, ambivalance, all those human tones coming through the tube.

Jim was very patriotic. I thought it only existed on the covers of *Newsweek* and *Time*. But no, if you take the train from New York to Chicago, there it is against a pumpkin-orange sunset, Three Mile Island. Jim stood up and saluted those three big towers, then sat back down.

Meanwhile I was trying to make a mild stand. I was trying to talk him out of his ideas. I don't know what my platform was—I mean, he was standing for all of America and I was just concerned for myself at that point. I really felt as if I were looking my death in the face. I'm not making up any of these stories, I'm really not. And if *he* was making up the story he was telling me, I figure he's white, and if he wants it bad enough and he's in the Navy, if he wasn't down in that waterproof chamber then, he must be down there now.

"Jim, Jim," I said, "you don't want to do it. Remember what happened to the guy who dropped the bomb on Hiroshima? He went crazy!"

"That asshole? He was not properly brainwashed. I," he said with great pride, "have been properly brainwashed. Also there is the nuclear destruct club. Do you think I'm the only one who's going to be pressing that green button? There's a whole bunch of us going to do it."

"Wait, wait, wait. You, all of you, don't want to die, do you? You're going to die if you push that button. Think of all you have to live for." I had to think hard about this one. "The blue-flake cocaine, for instance. Getting picked up by couples. The Swedish whores. Blowing away the cobwebs between your wife's legs. I mean, really."

"No, I'm not going to die. We get 'pubs.' "

Everything was abbreviated, and "pubs" meant Navy publications that tell them where to go to avoid radiation. And I could see him down there, after the rest of us have all been vaporized. He'll be down there in Tasmania or New Zealand starting this new red-faced, pea-brained, small-eared humanoid race. And I thought, the Mother needs a rest, Mother Earth needs a long, long rest.

If we're lucky he'll end up in Africa.

Anyway, he was beginning to realize that I wasn't totally on his side. It was hard to see that because I didn't have as detailed a platform as he had. Finally, he turned to me and said, "Listen Mr. Spalding," (I think by then he was calling me Gary Spalding) "you would not be doing that thing you do, writing, talking, whatever it is you do in the theatre, if it were not for me and the United States Navy stopping the Russians from taking over the world."

And I thought, wait a minute, maybe he's right. Maybe the Russians *are* trying to take over the world. Maybe *I'm* the one who's brainwashed. Maybe I've been hanging out with liberals too long. I mean, after all this time I thought I was a conscientious pacifist but maybe I've been deluding myself. Maybe I'm just a passive-aggressive unconscious coward, and like any good liberal, I should question everything. For instance, when did I last make a stand, any kind of stand, about anything? When did I just stand up for something right? Let alone America. What is America? Every time I try to think of America as a unit I get anxious. I think that's part of the reason I moved to Manhattan; I wanted to live on "an island off the coast of America." I wanted to live somewhere between America and Europe, a piece of land with very defined boundaries and only eight million people.

So I had no concept of America or of making a stand. I hated contact sports when I was a kid—I really didn't like the bumps. When I moved to New York City I wanted to be able to make a stand, so I took karate. But I had that horrid feeling of bone bouncing on bone whenever I hit my instructor or he hit me.

When I was in the seventh grade I fell in love with Judy Dorci. Butchy Coca was in love with her too. He lived on the other side of the tracks. He had a black leather motorcycle jacket and I had a camel's hair coat. I was careful never to go into his territory—I stayed in mine, Barrington, Rhode Island—but they didn't have a five-and-dime in Barrington and I had to buy Christmas presents. I went over to Warren, Rhode Island, Butchy's territory, to the five-and-dime, and one of Butchy's gang saw me—put the finger on me. I stepped outside and there they were, eight of them, like in *High Noon*, one foot up against the brick wall, smoking Chesterfield Regulars. I thought, this is it. I'm going to know what it's like to make a stand—but why rush it?

I ducked into the Warren Gazette just to look at Christmas cards, take my time, and there was Mr. Walker from Barrington. I said, "Hi, Mr. Walker, are you going my way?"

"I am. My car is out back. Do you mind going out the back door?"

"Nope. Let's go."

When I arrived in London for the first time, I was jet-lagging and I had to rent a car to go up to Edinburgh so I felt a little out of it. All right, I was driving on the wrong side of the road—easily done—you know, no big deal. I cut a guy off first thing, and when I rolled down the window to apologize, he said, "Take off those glasses, mate, I'm going to punch you out." Just like a British redcoat announcing his intentions ahead of time.

I just rolled up the window. Why rush it?

Last year I cut a man off on Hudson Street in Manhattan. I cut off a man from New Jersey, which is one of the worst things you can do. A man from New Jersey! And I rolled down the window—why I do this, I don't know—to apologize again. This time I saw the fist coming toward me and I thought, now I'll know what it's like to have my jaw broken in five places. At the last minute, just seconds before making contact with my face, he pulled the punch and hit the side of the van instead. He walked off with his knuckles bleeding, cursing. I rolled up the window and pulled out. Why rush it?

I had a friend who wanted to rush it, because he was going into the Army and he'd never been punched out. So he went to his friend Paul and said, "Paul, I've never been punched out. But I'm drafted, I'm going into the Army. Please punch me out Paul, quick." And Paul knocked him out.

I didn't want to go into the Army. I didn't want to get punched out. So I checked all the boxes. I admit it. I did it. I checked "homosexual" and "has trouble sleeping." Where it asked "What do you do when you can't sleep?" I put that I drank.

My mother was at home at the time having an incurable nervous breakdown and I was studying acting.

I thought that if worse came to worse I would just act the way she was acting and I'd get out of the Army. But there was a guy in front of me who looked very much like me; we both had beards. They touched him first, on the shoulder, and he just went bananas. He flipped out and they took him away screaming.

Now how was I going to follow that? I was depressed on two counts. One, it looked like I was going to be drafted, and two, it looked like I was a bad actor.

Recently in Manhattan, I was up early on a Sunday for some reason. It's rare. If you're up early in New York City on a Sunday, there's a strange overlap between those who are up early and those who haven't gone to bed yet. I was down in the Canal Street subway station—concrete no man's land. There were no subways coming, no law and order down there. There was just this one other guy and he was coming toward me. I knew he wanted something—I could feel the vibes. He needed something from me, wanted something. He was about to demand something.

"Hey man, you got change for a quarter?"

"Uh, yeah, I think I do. Here—wait a minute, I got two dimes here and one, two, three, four pennies. How's that?"

"Nope."

"Well, what are we going to do?"

"I got a quarter and a nickel. Got three dimes?"

"Yep, I do. Here." And I counted them out carefully in his hand.

He turned, walked away, then turned back to me and said, "You only gave me two dimes, man."

"Wait a minute. I'm very careful about money matters."

Now, was this where I was going to make my stand?

"Very well. If you feel you need another dime, here."

Renée has this upstairs neighbor who is a member of the Art Mafia. She has her own gallery in Soho, along with a drinking problem, and she is unbearable. She plays her quadrophonic machine at all hours, full blast, Bob Dylan's "Sarah," over and over again. Something must have happened to her way back when that song was popular and she can't get it out of her head. She comes in drunk, puts it on at 1:30 in the morning. Now if it was 1:30 every morning, it would be great. It would be like feeding time, you know. You could get through it. You'd get used to it. But it's 1:35 or it's 2:10 or it's 4:14. You call the police but it does no good. She turns it down, they leave, she turns it up. You call the police again, they come, she turns it down, they leave, she turns it up. What can you do? You can't go to the landlord—he's Italian Mafia and lives in New Jersey.

I don't know which Mafia I dislike the most. I'm leaning toward liking the Italian Mafia because they are just immoral and still believe in mother and child. But the Art Mafia is immoral and, from what I can tell, they've stopped procreating.

So we're in Renée's apartment and I call up, "Please stop persecuting us." And she sends down these young, new artists who have gotten rich and famous in New York, but are now camping out in sleeping bags until they find their niches. And they say, "Hey man. MAN. You know New York is Party City. That's why we

moved here. So we could have parties on weekday nights.
If you don't like it, move to the country—OLD MAN."

I try to practice my Buddhist Tolerance—I am turning all my cheeks to the wall at this point. I mean,
really, Buddhist Tolerance in New York is just one big
pacifist-escapist rationalization. Renée is not practic-
ing it. She is pacing while steam comes screaming out
of her navel.

Now there are some people who say that this woman
should be killed. And I find that I'm not saying no. I
don't protest it. They are talking about vigilantes.

I don't know the language. I knew the language when
I was with my people in Boston in 1962, in whitebread
homogeneous Boston, brick-wall Boston. In the old days,
when I spoke a common language with my people, they
had what was called the "hi-fi." And when the hi-fi
was too loud, all I had to do was call up and say, "Hi,
Puffy. Spuddy Gray, down here. Yeah. You guessed it.
The hi-fi is a little loud. Yeah. I wouldn't say anything
but I've got an early dance class in the morning. Great.
Thanks a lot. Yeah, Merry Christmas to you too, Puff."
Down it would go. You see I knew the language.

Now Renée knows the language because her father
was in the Jewish Mafia. So she calls up, "Bet you want
to die, right? Bitch! Bitch! Cunt! I'll beat your fucking
face in with a baseball bat. Bitch!" And she slams down
the phone. The music gets louder.

One day I was walking out the door carrying an empty
bottle of Molson Golden. I guess I was going to get my
nickel back. And I heard this party noise coming from
upstairs and I was seized with gut rage. Maybe I'd had
a few drinks and the rage finally made it to my gut.

Not that my intellect wasn't still working—it was going like a ticker tape, repeating that old adage, "All weakness tends to corrupt, and impotence corrupts absolutely." I just took the bottle and *hurled* it—my arm practically came out of its socket. It went up the flight of stairs, hit the door and exploded like a hand grenade. They charged out with their bats and guns. I ran. Because it was an act of passion, I had forgotten to tell Renée I was going to do it and she was behind me, picking up some plastic garbage bags or something. She was way behind me so when they got to her door they met up with her. But she was innocent and they recognized that. They recognized that she was truly innocent and they didn't kill her. So there's hope.

But I wonder, how do we begin to approach the so-called Cold War (or Now-Heating-Up War) between Russia and America if I can't even begin to resolve the Hot War down on Northmoor and Greenwich in lower Manhattan?

When I was in therapy about two years ago, one day I noticed that I hadn't had any children. And I like children at a distance. I wondered if I'd like them up close. I wondered why I didn't have any. I wondered if it was a mistake, or if I'd done it on purpose, or what. And I noticed that my therapist didn't have any children either. He had pictures of cats on the wall. Framed.

He may have changed since then, but my therapist was the kind who, if you asked him a personal question, would take the entire session to answer. You had to take the responsibility to stop him. You had to learn to be selfish. So I always said that he was like a drinking partner, except we never went drinking and I paid for the drinks.

I asked him, "Why didn't you ever have any children?"

And he said, "Well, I was in Auschwitz when I was nineteen and the death marches were moving out as the Russians moved in. And I said to my friend, who was also nineteen, 'I think now we have a beneficent Gestapo. Now we must run for it.' And my friend said, 'No, I am too tired. I must first rest.' So I am watching him sleeping and I see blood from the corner of his mouth and I realize he is dead from exhaustion. So I run and escape and I make it to the border of Poland and Germany, and another death march of twenty thousand goes by, not so beneficent this time. They are shooting from horseback, and I surrender.

"They take us to the edge of this great pit and machine gun the whole lot of us. Everyone falls dead except maybe some twelve or fifteen who fall into the snow and live. I am one. I am shot in and around the genitals so it's a kind of automatic vasectomy. Two days later the Russians find me in the snow."

I said, "Two days in the snow and you didn't freeze to death?"

"What . . . ," he answered, "it was just *snow*." (And *I* was the one in therapy?)

"Listen, this is going to sound weird, but I really envy you."

"What, are you one of those who think suffering ennobles?"

"No, it's not that. We're all born by chance, no one asked to get born, but to be reborn by chance, to live like that, it must have made your life—you know—

much more conscious and vital. Things must have changed enormously for you. Also, you don't have to make a decision about whether or not to have kids. It must have changed your life in a very dynamic . . ."

"No. Uh-uh. Nothing changes, no. We thought that, you see. In the first reunions of the camps everyone was swinging, like a big sex club with the swinging and the drinking and the carrying on as though you die tomorrow. Everyone did what he wanted. The next time, not so much, not so much. The couples stayed together. The next time, we were talking about whether or not we could afford a summer home that year. Now when we meet, years later, people talk about whether or not radioactive smoke-detectors are dangerous in suburban homes. Nothing changes."

So I got the role and I went to Bangkok. The only thing that I knew about Bangkok was that my hero Thomas Merton had died there. Thomas Merton was a hero of mine because he knew how to shut up. It's not that he wanted other people to stop talking, but he figured that people were chatting so much that someone had to keep the silence. He believed in the silence. And he believed in the power of silent prayer, so he became a Trappist. He got interested in Buddhism and the Trappists sent him to Southeast Asia to research Buddhism. He stepped out of a bathtub, touched an electric fan and died instantly. Judith Malina said it was a CIA plot but I don't know. I don't know.

I arrived in this city, 200 years old, 110 degrees, built on a swamp and sinking, and under my door was pushed this letter from Enigma Films—with the "a" upside

down—addressed to Spalding Gray, Esquire. It was my
first major film for a British company—they spoiled me
rotten. They referred to all of the actors as "artists."
They can get you to do anything that way.

The letter was dated May 6, 1983 and was from David
Puttnam, the producer:

Dear Spalding,
On Sunday we all start to make a very difficult but
worthwhile film. It is by far and away the most
ambitious that I have ever attempted to produce,
and it will, by the time we get through, have thor-
oughly tested us all. I'm sure that, like me, you
constantly get asked what movies you've worked
on. I always *hope* that the one I'm presently working on will instantly top the list when answering
that question. All too often it doesn't work out that
way. However, by nature, by sheer scope and theme,
The Killing Fields is one of those few movies by
which all our careers will undoubtedly be judged.
Roland and I found a speech of President Kennedy's this week in which he said, 'I realize that
the pursuit of peace is not as dramatic as the pursuit of war. And frequently the words of the pursuer
fall on deaf ears. But we have no more urgent task.'
Those words, spoken twenty years ago, have never
been more relevant. We have a unique opportunity
with this film to make our contribution. In the
years to come, it is my honest belief that *The Killing Fields* will be the very first we mention in ex-
plaining and justifying the way we spent the best
and most difficult years of our lives.

For my part, I'll always be around to help if things go ugly. But in the final analysis all I can do is stand back, support Roland to the hilt and hope that luck and good sense run with us. All the best to all of us. This story deserves to be told and told well. If we pull that off then every form of possible reward will undoubtedly follow, and we will deserve it.

David Puttnam

My first big scene was to be filmed on a soccer field outside of Bangkok. We were reenacting the 1975 evacuation of the American embassy in Phnom Penh. I was with Ira Wheeler, who was playing John Gunther Dean, the last American ambassador.

Ira is an interesting man—he used to be vice president of American Celanese Chemical. After he retired he was singing in a glee club in New York, where someone saw him and put him in Jane Fonda's *Rollover*. Now, at sixty-three years old, he was beginning his film career. If you live long enough I find it all comes full circle. Shortly after I arrived in Bangkok I found out that Ira served on the same ship in World War II as my Uncle Tinky. They were on an LST together in the Pacific.

So Ira was playing John Gunther Dean, the last American ambassador. We got to meet Dean because he is now ambassador to Thailand, right there in Bangkok. And because Costa Gavras was getting sued for fourteen million dollars by the Chilean ambassador for *Missing*, David Puttnam wasn't taking any chances. He

37

was bending over backwards to have the text examined
by the ambassador to make sure it represented history
the way he remembered it.

Ira and I went over to visit him because we wanted
to meet a real ambassador. I was very intimidated by
this man. I had met politicians but never a *statesman*.
And he was a true statesman, a combination of a ship's
captain, say, of the Q.E. II, and a boarding school prin-
cipal, say, of Phillips or Andover Academy. And he said,
"We saw Cambodia as a ship floundering in high seas.
We wanted desperately to bring her safely into port.
When we saw we were going to lose her, we wanted to
leave the ship with dignity, and I cut down the American flag that you see behind me, wrapped it in plastic
and carried it over my arm."

And there we were, Ira running with the American
flag wrapped in plastic over his arm. And me, the ambassador's aide, running beside him, heading for a Cadillac limousine parked on the soccer field. We got to
the Cadillac limousine, it was 110 degrees, and the first
thing that happened was that the air conditioner broke.
We had to spend the whole day in this black torture
box—it was going to take that long to shoot the scene—
and Ira was sweating, he was dripping. It was cooler
outside than in, and Ira is the type who sweats like a,
like . . . an *Ira*. He sweats so much that he says he beats
his opponents at squash because they slip in his puddles.

Wardrobe was changing his shirt while we sat in the
limousine and next the electric windows broke, the
radiator boiled over and by the end of the day the entire
exhaust system and muffler were dragging on the football field. I was laughing—I found the whole thing very
funny. Roland Joffe had told us, "Look like you're on

the verge of tears." Ira, who was studying Stanislavsky acting for the first time and had read *An Actor Prepares* and *Building a Character*, thought that Roland meant "on the verge of tears" *all day long*, just in case the camera was turned on. So he was doing an emotional memory and he was in a deep funk. You couldn't even approach him.

I was so bored that I began talking to the driver—an extra. He was an expatriate from San Francisco, an elephant expert, who was spending his time counting elephants in the Thai jungle because he thought, "America is going crazy. Going nuts, going to the dogs. Going to the wow-wows." He went to Thailand to get his sanity back, and in Thailand he only trusted elephants. So they were all he was interested in. He slept in the bush at night and in the morning he got up, grabbed his elephant counter and just counted elephants.

He had a limp, a game leg—and he knew that if you frighten elephants at night they will charge. They sleep standing up and he was sure, he confided to me, that he was going to be killed within the following two months by a stampeding elephant.

In the middle of this Ira looked up and cried out, "WILL YOU STOP TALKING ABOUT WHATEVER IT IS YOU'RE TALKING ABOUT? I'm trying to have an emotional memory."

"Ira, Ira, this guy is about to be killed by an elephant, for *real*. Think on *that*."

And we were driving through this black smoke, pouring up off of rubber tires, which were burning to make it look like a real war. We headed for a nonexistent Sikorski—I guess because the American Air Force had not given the Thai Air Force any Sikorskis. They just had little choppers. We were supposed to be getting into the Sikorski but we were just pretending it was there. We drove through Marine guards, lots of extras dressed as American Marines—I don't know who those guys were. I think some of them were Marines who didn't get enough of the war so they went back to join up with Bo Gritz, who had a foreign legion going in Laos to look for MIAs. Others were there to deal drugs, which is extremely lucrative but very dangerous in Thailand. And still others were there basically for the sex. Because on one lower Chakra level Bangkok is one big whorehouse. It's not all our fault, or the fault of the troops on R&R, or the Japanese sex tourists. The tradition existed way back before the war, when there were concubines in all the villages. It just got way out of hand during the war. They had hundreds of prostitutes in quonset huts the size of airplane hangars, to service all the soldiers—and for birth control they took Chinese herbal potions. There were a lot of Amerasian children being born.

After the Vietnam war they put all the prostitutes in Pat Pong. If you've been to Bangkok you've probably seen Pat Pong. (There's nothing else to see in Bangkok but the Gold Buddha. You can see the Gold Buddha during the day and Pat Pong at night.) If you've seen the film *The Deer Hunter*, you've seen Pat Pong; all of the Saigon sequences were shot there, at the Mississippi Queen. The Mississippi Queen is still there, and walking into it is like stepping into that film.

There is no sense of seduction, as in "across a crowded

room." The whores just fly to you and stick, and they're small enough that your body can carry six at once, two on an elbow, two on a lap, two here, two there, until you feel like a Christmas tree. You just sit there and they go wild. They smile, giggle, reach into your pockets, and if you can make up your mind which one you're in love with by one o'clock, which is closing time, you can go home with her. Or, if you have enough money, you can go home with all of them. Each one costs 500 Thai *bhat* (about twenty-six dollars) for the entire evening. If you want to buy her out early you can pay another 300 *bhat* and go home anytime. You can even walk to the hotel to save money.

If you don't want to spend the whole night with a giggly, happy Thai whore driving you nuts, or if you're afraid of the intimacies involved and would rather be in control, you can go instead to a massage parlor. The massage parlors are very much like huge department stores; there are three floors. You go in and there are, maybe, thirty-five women on one floor, behind a one-way glass, all fully clothed under fluorescent lighting, sitting on tiers and wearing numbers. All of them are looking at a focal point just under the partition. You don't know what they're looking at, but it's a TV. They're all watching TV.

So you strut up and down in front of that glass like a little Sultan until at last you think you've found the perrrr-fect body, suppose it's Number Eight. You say to the man, "Could you call Number Eight for me, please?"

And he calls over a microphone, "Numbah Eight."

Number Eight stands up and you can tell by her disgruntled expression that it's not going to be as great as you had thought, because you've interrupted her TV show.

You go down into this small room and for a little bit of money you take off all your clothes and she stays dressed, and you get a mild, tweek-tweek massage; nothing Reichian about it. A mild, tweek-tweek surface massage. And for a little bit more money she takes off all her clothes and gives you another mild, tweek-tweek surface massage, and occasionally you might feel her warm, brown Thai body brush-brush up against yours. A little bit more money and you get a hand job. A little bit more money and you get to fuck her. A little bit more money and you get the supremo-supremo . . . the body-body massage. For the body-body massage she puts you in a tub and she completely soaps you up. She doesn't rinse you. She puts you, slippery, on a waterbed. Then she gets in the tub and soaps herself up so she's slippery too, and she doesn't rinse herself either. And she gets on one side of the room and runs and hops on top of you and goes swiggle-swiggle-swiggle, body-body-body, and you slide together like two very wet bars of soap. For the final facial massage she'll let you put your face between her breasts, she'll part them and then let them go and cry out "Boobily-oobily!"

After you've been fucked, sucked, had your tubes cleaned, toes cleaned and nose cleaned and you're ready for more, you can go rest and relax at a live show. At a live show the women do everything with their vaginas except have babies. One starts with ping-pong balls and a soda fountain glass: Chung, chung, chung, she catches the ball in the glass. Then another brings out a Coca-Cola bottle, a king-size Coke, which she shakes for a long time, really shakes it hard. She works on it and

42

works on it for a long time until—I don't know how, but she does it—she opens it. I don't know if she has a bottle opener in there, or teeth, but the Coke sprays all over the audience (because it's warm, and she's shaken it). Then she pours the rest of the Coke into her womb, squats and—whoosh—refills the bottle like a Coca-Cola bottling machine.

Then comes the banana. First she shoots a few lame shots, just boring shots like those Russian rockets that are going to sputter and pop and land on our cornfields. One, two, three. Then, for the finale, she aims her vagina down the center aisle like a cannon, loads it with a very ripe banana and—FOOP!—fires it. She almost hit me in the eye, almost hit an Australian housewife in the head. The banana hits the back wall and sticks, then slowly slides down to the floor where it is devoured by an army of giant roaches.

For the last act, out comes a Thai couple to do a live sex show. They do all the *kama sutra* poses—and the Thais are the most beautiful race of people I've ever seen. When you see them coming toward you on a Bangkok street you don't know whether they're men or women; there is such androgyny afoot. And when they get closer to you it doesn't matter. The couple does this live fuck show as if they're dancing. They are so beautiful as they go through their poses and positions. And they end with her completely wrapped around him, belly up, in this incredible contortion. And he's got his dick deep in her to hold her up, as she balances in a classic praying position, watching a rerun of *Poltergeist* on the TV over the bar and waving to her friends. Then it's time to go home.

Now some men have no problems with all of this,

men who can admit to a longing for the old Henry Miller days. I know I'm too ambivalent about it to count myself in. In fact, some of the British actors said I was resisting tradition, that the whores were there for me and that I should go to them. That was a rule of the culture. But I was ambivalent about it. I found it very difficult to just leap in and not think about it. But the man who wants to, who knows the power balances he would like, who knows that if the bomb doesn't go off, the sun will go out eventually so therefore he's not concerned with history, who knows that after he dies his history will last maybe twenty minutes at most, who just wants to regress a little bit, that man should go to Thailand for a vacation. But he should be careful because it inflates your estrogen and ego in the worst way, making it difficult to reenter the West. He may end up staying on as a schoolteacher—many men do. They get stuck in the Lust Ring. I met them there and they were schoolteachers.

Now one of the American actors in the film was determined not to get stuck in this Lust Ring, and to be loyal to his wife back in the States. He just didn't want to get stuck in a situation of lust, so he worked out his libido by jogging and playing tennis. On the third or fourth day out jogging, he pulled a muscle in his right leg very badly, and in our hotel—which was like a Ramada Inn—he saw a sign for massage. He figured it was on the up and up, as it were. He asked for the "regular massage."

Later, he said, "I went in, my God, they worked on

the wrong muscle for an hour! For an hour I got a hand job; where am I going to get my leg fixed in this town?" You see, it's subtle.

We were in the posh lounge of this Ramada Inn-like hotel. The only difference between it and a Ramada Inn was that it had those *King and I* round windows to make it Siamese. There was this woman singing with a Thai combo, "*Killing me softly with his song . . .*" and we were ordering Kloster beers. "*Killing me softly . . .*" and rats, posh rats, were running across the wall-to-wall carpeted bar to hide up under the furniture. "*Killing me softly . . .*" and the Art Department was coming through with Cambodian body parts, artificial limbs for the film. Skeletons, skulls, legs, bones, then "*Killing me softly . . .*"

The waitress was on her way over with two beers, slinking and dancing, three inches off the carpet. And she had a slit up the side of her skirt so you could see her naked leg flashing through. She came to deliver the two beers, slid in and knelt at our feet, took the beers off her tray and put them on the coffee table. It's subtle.

We were out by the pool and this woman came out, May. We called her Chang Mai May. She said, "Dear sirs, I can't read this writing. Can you please read this letter to me?"

It said, "Dear May: I will be arriving from Saudi Arabia on Friday. I trust your judgment implicitly. I hope you have a lovely escort waiting for me in my room. If I like her I will marry her. She must be prepared to return to Saudi Arabia where she'll spend the next six months, at which time we'll move to London where she will spend the rest of her life."

By the way, marriage is a very simple thing in Thailand. It's a verbal agreement. It can be done in a telephone booth, a swimming pool, a bed, on the beach, wherever. But I'm told that when Thai women marry foreigners and get taken out of the country, they don't stay very long wherever it is that they're taken. They miss Thailand and go back.

I am also told that Thai wives are very jealous. If one of them ever catches her husband with another woman, when he least expects it she cuts off his cock with a straight-edged razor and feeds it to the ducks. (When I first heard this I thought it was a joke, but since then I've heard otherwise.) Thai husbands have gotten so used to this behavior now that they've learned to run and get the severed penis out of the duck's throat— before it's swallowed up—and get it to a new plastic surgical penis transplant wing that Thai hospitals have. In order to beat this, the Thai wives are now beginning to tie the penises onto gas balloons and send them up in the backyard.

So there we were, driving through the black smoke and Marine guards, heading for a Sikorski that didn't exist. We got to where the Sikorski was supposed to be and, "Cut." End of shot.

Five months later, when the filming was over, they located the Sikorskis—at Camp Pendleton in San Diego. That was the only place they could find any. So we went down there for one last shoot—it was incredible.

The pyrotechies were running around pulling those same rubber tires, sending up black smoke, but this time the crew had tee-shirts on that read "SKIP THE DIALOGUE, LET'S BLOW SOMETHING UP."

So there we were on this Marine base, the actors, these Thai kids who were playing Dith Pran's children who had been flown in from Bangkok for the day, and the Marines, who were very excited. It was the day after the Beirut Massacre and they weren't even talking about Beirut. Their flags weren't even at half-mast. (Actually, I figured out why that was. California American flags are the largest American flags in the world. If they were put at half-mast they'd drag on the ground. California also seems to have the smallest flag poles in relation to the size of the flag.)

The Marines were thrilled to have real actors on the base.

"Craig T. Nelson? *Big Chill*, I know it. Don't say no. I saw you in *The Big Chill*."

"Tom Bird? *Love Is a Many Splendored Thing*. I'm sure I saw you in that. Don't say no."

So we weren't saying no. We were milling around, talking about what it was like to be a star, giving autographs, when over the horizon came these three giant birds. These Sikorskis are really big. And the Marines turned as though they'd rehearsed it and, on cue, sang the "tune" from *Apocalypse Now*, you know, *The Ride of the Valkyries*, "ba-BA-ba-ba-BAA-ba, ba-BA-ba-ba-BAAA-ba . . ." as the helicopters came in and landed. We got on one of them with the wind blowing and the black smoke, and in the finished film it only lasts about thirty seconds. I got on with Ira Wheeler, but then we had to get right off again because we weren't allowed to take off. Only the Marines who were playing Marines were.

One of the Marine guards who had escorted us onto the helicopter got a Polaroid picture of the scene from Continuity and asked us, "Would you please sign this picture for me? I want to send it to my folks in North Carolina. Because if I never do anything else in my life, at least I can say I have done this."

The actual evacuation of Phnom Penh took place on April 12, 1975. Lon Nol had long since fled to Hawaii and there were two million people in the capital instead of the usual six hundred thousand. There was no food. Khmer Rouge rockets were coming in and landing in the streets, on schools, randomly. At six o'clock in the morning John Gunther Dean put out a letter to all American and Cambodian officials, notifying them that the evacuation was taking place: "You have two-and-a-half hours to make it here to the embassy and then we're taking off."

The Prime Minister of Cambodia Long Boret said, "Two-and-a-half hours? How are we going to convince the Russians that we're Socialists in two-and-a-half hours? We're ruined."

Long Boret, Lon Non and Prince Sirik Matak stayed behind. By the way, Lon Nol had two brothers, Lon Non and Lon Nil. Lon Nil was killed in an early insurrection and they cut out his liver and rushed it to a Chinese restaurant, cooked it up in a wok and fed it to the people in the streets. The Khmers were really big on the powers of the human liver.

Prince Sirik Matak sent a letter to the American ambassador informing him that they were not going to evacuate. It read:

Dear Excellency and Friend,
I thank you very sincerely for your letter and for your offer to transport me toward freedom. I cannot, alas, leave in such a cowardly fashion. As for you, and in particular for your great country, I never believed for a moment that you would have the sentiment of abandoning a people which has chosen liberty. You have refused us your protection and we can do nothing about it. You leave, and it is my wish that you and your country will find happiness under the sky. But mark it well, that if I shall die here on the spot, and in the country that I love, it is too bad because we are all born and must one day die. I have only committed this mistake of believing in you, the Americans. Please accept, Excellency, my dear friend, my faithful and friendly sentiments.

Sirik Matak

Five days later their livers were carried through the streets on sticks.

The Americans thought it would be like Danang during the evacuation, but it wasn't. There was no rioting, there were no people hanging off the helicopter runners like in Vietnam. The Cambodians just waved and called, "Okay, bye-bye. Okay, bye-bye." They were still smiling. The last helicopter took off and a Khmer Rouge rocket came in and killed one of the people watching. Five days later, April 17, 1975, it was "Cambodia Year Zero."

In marched the Khmer Rouge in their black pajamas and Lon Nol's troops threw down their guns and raced to embrace them, thinking that the country would then be reunited. The Khmer Rouge did not smile back. They took strategic points in the city. Some of the kids, because they had grown up in the jungle and never seen cars before, were jumping into cars, getting stuck in first gear and ramming them into buildings. There was chaos for awhile, but soon order reigned. And the Khmer Rouge said, "*Out.* Everyone out of the city. The Americans are going to bomb Phnom Penh. Get out. There's no more food, so *out.* Who will take care of you? *Angka* will provide. *Angka* is out there, so get out of the city. *Angka . . .*" like some sort of perverse Wizard of Oz figure, "*Angka . . .*" like some Kafkaesque thundercloud raining down manna to feed the people. They emptied a city of two million people in twenty-four hours.

Those who were in hospitals, who couldn't walk, were just chucked out the window, no matter which story they were on. Out the window. Survival of the fittest. Then the mass murder began. Eyewitnesses said that everyone who had any kind of education was killed. Any artist, any civil servant was butchered. Anyone wearing glasses was killed. The only hope was to convince them that you were a cab driver, so suddenly there were a thousand more cab drivers than cabs. It was just the opposite of New York, where everyone says, "I'm an artist, I'm an artist. Sure, I drive a cab to make a living, but I'm really an *artist.*" There if you were an artist, boom, you became dead. Little kids were doing the killing, ten-year-olds, fifteen-year-olds. There was very little ammunition left so they were beating people over the head with ax handles or hoses or whatever they could get hold of. Some of the skulls were too tough for sticks and clubs, and because the kids were weak from eating only bark, bugs, leaves and lizards, they often didn't have the strength to kill. So to make it more fun, they were taking bets on how many whacks it would take to cave in a head.

Some eyewitnesses said that the kids were laughing with a demented glee. And if you pleaded for mercy they laughed harder. If you were a woman pleading for mercy they laughed even harder. And if you didn't die the kids just took your half-dead body and threw it in an American bomb crater, which acted as a perfect grave. It was a kind of hell on earth.

You were killed if you had your own cooking pot. It was better to kill an innocent person, the Khmer Rouge said, than to leave an enemy alive. It was nothing like the methodical, scientific German genocide. They were tearing apart little children like fresh bread in front of their mothers, gouging out eyes, cutting open pregnant women. And this went on for four years. Two million people were either killed outright or starved to death. And to this day no one knows exactly what happened, what caused this kind of mad autogenocide to come into being. Oh sure, it's easy to research what happened in Germany because we can speak German, and Hitler's dead or living in Argentina. But Pol Pot is recognized by the United States government. And he's still out there, waiting.

We don't know what happened because the Vietnamese invaded Cambodia in 1979 and *they* say it was a liberation. Others say it was a piece of cake, a xenophobic piece of cake. They invaded in '79 and now they're writing their own revisionist history. We don't know what went on. Maybe a cloud of evil did land and the people simply went mad.

But whatever was going on, Pol Pot is still alive and up there and waiting to return. He's protected by the United States and the United Nations, and the Red Cross brings him food. And he's fighting the Vietnamese up there, the people who originally taught *him* to fight. Roland Joffe said to me, "My God, Spalding, morality is not a moveable feast." But I keep seeing it moving, all the time.

My last big scene was with Sam Waterston in Waheen, Gulf of Siam. Not at the Pleasure Prison, where we were sleeping, but at this beautiful Victorian hotel in Waheen that they had emptied out for the film because it looked like the Hotel Phnom Penh. The only thing that made it inauthentic was that it didn't have a swimming pool or a tennis court. So the film built a swimming pool and a tennis court.

Now what I haven't told you is that the American Air Force had what it called "homing beacons" on the ground. And when the planes flew over, six miles up, they could take a radar coordinate off those homing beacons and then the navigator threw a switch and all the bombs were dropped over the target by computer. So no one really dropped a bomb from six miles up; it was done on automatic. The beacons were everywhere. There was one on the American embassy. There was also one in Neak Luong, and on August 7, 1973, a navigator made a mistake. He threw his switch at the wrong time and dropped an entire load of bombs on this strategic ferry town, Neak Luong. The navigator was fined $700 for the mistake.

Sidney Schanberg told me that he heard about it and went up to cover it for *The New York Times*. But the American embassy had put an absolute press lock on the whole area; no one was allowed in. Sidney bribed his way in, snuck his way in with Dith Pran, and they paid people to get them there. He told me that he reached Neak Luong about two days after the accident, and that all the dead had been removed, but he saw blood and hair all over the bushes and speculated that more than 200 people had been killed. He told me the Cambodians put him under "polite house arrest," so he couldn't break his story to the *Times*.

During the time he was under guard, the American embassy flew in officials to give out hundred-dollar bills to people who had lost family in the bombing, fifties to people who had lost arms or legs. And the Cambodians were grateful.

Sidney told me that he had the feeling he could just walk out if he wanted to; the Cambodians wouldn't shoot him in front of American embassy officials, he was pretty sure. As he started to walk, he heard the safeties on their guns click and men start screaming, "Stop." He said, "This may sound strange, but I'd never felt more alive in my life than when I was right on the edge of death. I never felt more alive!"

Elizabeth Becker told me the same thing. She was reporting for the *Washington Post* and a colleague of hers was killed by the Khmer Rouge in the house they lived

53

in. She felt remorse for her colleague but also an enormous sense of being alive. She told me about it as we sat on the steps of her Washington house drinking white wine, eating pâté with white bread. And I was listening but I wasn't looking at her. Instead I was watching some black ants crawl across the brick walk to eat this small piece of pâté that had fallen there. And into my frame of vision came Elizabeth's hand, holding a white linen napkin. She just reached down and wiped out the entire trail of ants with one sweep of her hand. I appeared to be listening to her but inside I was weeping, *oh my God, all those ants, all those innocent ants dead for no reason at all.*

Now what I had to say in my scene with Sam was simple—it was a little technical, but simple: "A computer malfunction put out the wrong set of coordinates. Seems a single B-52 opened up over Neak Luong. There's a homing beacon right in the middle of town. Check it out, Sid."

All right. Simple enough . . . for some actors. But *this* actor needs images for technical words like that. I have to build my own internal film, you see, or I can't remember the words.

By the way, I played one of those American officials who flew into Neak Luong. We were at an old garbage dump that they had made into Neak Luong, right outside Bangkok. The assistant director said, "Would the artists please get on the choppers." Now there is no way I would ordinarily get on a helicopter, but he called me an artist and hop, hop, I was right on that chopper like Pavlov's dog. They said it was only going to go up ten feet and then just land. All they needed was a shot of the embassy officials jumping off the choppers.

So I got on the helicopter and it went BRRRRRRRRR— straight up. Straight up above this incredible jungle. I felt like I was in a movie, like I was in *Apocalypse Now*, and then I realized that I *was* in a movie! They were filming me, and I had no fear, even though the door was wide open and I was looking down. Craig T. Nelson was practically falling out the door—we had no safety belts—but I suddenly had no fear because the camera eroticizes the space! It protects you like Colgate Guard-All. Even if the chopper crashed, at least there would be rushes, right? My friends could show them on New Year's Eve at the Performing Garage.

We went up six times and the feeling was triumphant. I was looking up the Chao Phraya River and I saw, my God, how much area the film controlled! Twenty square miles of Thai jungle, all the way up the river, there were Thai peasants throwing more rubber tires on the fire to make black smoke, to make it look like war, and I thought, of course! WAR THERAPY. Every country should make a major war movie every year. It would put a lot of people to work, help them get their rocks off. And when you land in that jungle you don't have to Method-act. When those helicopter blades are whirring overhead, you shout to be heard. You don't have to Method-act when you look down and see a Thai peasant covered with chicken giblets and fake blood in 110-degree weather for fifteen hours a day for five dollars a day. (If they're real amputees they get seven-fifty.) It's just like the real event!

So, "a computer malfunctioned." I had an image of a computer in my mind, spaghetti coming out of it—a malfunction. "Put out the wrong coordinates . . . ," for coordinates I had an image of an oscillator from a seventh-grade science project, I don't remember who had one, but it was a grid-work oscillator. "It seems a single B-52 . . . ," I remembered B-52s from many drunken dinners in front of the TV during That War. "Opened up over Neak Luong . . . ," I was having trouble with Neak Luong. It was a night shoot and I was a little hung over. At times I was calling it Luong Neak. I was a little shaky from that heavy party the night before, and the dose of marijuana and booze. But I didn't feel too bad about it because Roland told me that my character would be drinking a lot because he was very guilty. So I thought, to some extent, I was in character.

You would be amazed at what some people went through to get in character for this film. For instance, John Malkovich seemed to be in character all the time. He was the same on camera as off, and I couldn't figure it out. So I went to him and asked him, "John, are you one of those actors who are in character all the time?" And he just said, "No, Spalding, not at all." I was a little confused but I finally figured out that John Malkovich's character was the kind of character who would say he wasn't in character when he really was.

There was one British actor, a suburban guy from outside London with a wife and family, who seemed to be *living* his character in the streets of Bangkok. He was convinced that his character would fall in love with a *Mamasan*, one of the women who run dance halls in Pat Pong. So he did. He started to actually fall in love with one, and to believe that he ran the night club with her. And then he started thinking that he would stay behind after the film was finished and open his own club in Pat Pong. His wife kept calling up, asking, "Where's my husband?" At last she said, "You got him over there, you get him back." It took four people to get him on that plane back to London. He said it wasn't until he was halfway back that he realized he'd gone mad.

"Okay, boys and girls, let's go. Take sixty-four."

It was a night shoot and we were up to take sixty-four. And it was just the first scene of the night. I thought I had it down. "A computer malfunction put out the wrong set of coordinates. It seems a single B-52 opened up over Neak Luong. There's a . . ." and I couldn't get the image of the homing beacon. I said, "There's a *housing device* right in the middle of town."

"CUT. Okay, let's go back. Keep it together now."

I don't know why I was feeling under so much pressure. I had already done my worst scene. It was one that was cut from the film, in which 888 Thai marching troops passed in front of what was supposed to be Lon Nol's reviewing stand. They were real Thai army troops playing Cambodians, and when the drummer got to my shoulder I was to be seen leaking information to Sam Waterston. When the drummer got to my shoulder I missed my cue. In 110 degrees, 888 troops had to march all the way back. It took about twenty minutes. Then

Sam missed a cue. Then something went wrong with the camera. It took six takes, and by the sixth take, far into the day, I saw these troops coming at me and an insidious voice inside me was whispering, "You're going to miss it, you're going to miss it, you're going to miss it." Now who is that voice? And what is that voice? That's all I want to know.

"Okay, boys and girls, let's go. Take sixty-five."

"A computer malfunction put out the wrong set of coordinates. It seems a single B-52 opened up over Luong . . . over Neak . . . sorry."

"All right, Spalding. Take sixty-six."

At last I had the image for homing beacon. I saw a pigeon, a homing pigeon, flying toward a lighthouse beacon in a children's storybook. Got it.

"Let's go. Take sixty-six."

"A computer malfunction put out the wrong set of coordinates. It seems a single B-52 opened up over Neak Luong. There's a . . ." and I knew it would work. It didn't matter what I was thinking, so long as I was thinking something. Because everyone looking at the film would be thinking their own thoughts and projecting them on me

"There's a homing beacon right in the middle of town. Check it out, Sid."

The entire crew burst into applause. Sixty-six takes later and five hours into the night we had finished the first scene of the evening. And I was told that it would cost $30,000 to process it, including the cost of the film and crew. Then, when I got back to New York, I was called in to redub the entire scene anyway, because of the sound of crickets. So what you hear in the film is my voice in New York City, reacting to some black-

and-white footage shot one hot summer night on the Gulf of Siam.

A private car was waiting for us and Renée and I were driven back to the Pleasure Prison. As we rode along I was thinking, "Why do I feel so inflated, so pumped up, so on edge? I have been here eight weeks and worked only eight days." I mean, talk about mad dogs and Englishmen, the British were incredible. A sixty-year-old makeup man stood for hours each day in the burning sun, just to press ice packs on our necks so we wouldn't faint, and *I* was complaining? I was feeling ravaged, all spoiled and puffed up. But, oh, how I was going to miss it. How I was going to miss it.

Riding in the car, I said a silent farewell. Farewell to the fantastic breakfasts, the pineapple like I'd never tasted and probably never will taste again. Farewell to the fresh mango and papaya, farewell to the Thai maid and the fresh, clean, cotton sheets on the king-size bed every night. Farewell to the incredible free lunches under the circus tent with fresh meat flown in from America every day. Roast lamb, roast potatoes and green beans at 110 degrees, in accordance with British Equity. Farewell to the cakes and teas and ices at four. Farewell to the Thai driver with the tinted glasses and the Mercedes with the one-way windows. Farewell to the single fresh rose in the glass on my bureau every morning.

And just as I was dozing off in the Pleasure Prison, I had a flash. An inkling. I suddenly thought I knew what it was that killed Marilyn Monroe.

part two

▽   ▽   ▽   ▽   ▽   ▽   ▽

▽   ▽   ▽   ▽,   ▽   ▽

So I told Renée that I would be back by the eighth of July or as soon as I had a Perfect Moment, whichever occurred first.

Now, I thought it would be all right, I thought I would be able to make it back, but . . . all of a sudden I realized I had an open ticket on the airplane, and the last time I had an open ticket was in 1976 when I was in India, and I was almost hospitalized for not being able to make up my mind.

I thought I had grown up since then, I thought I had developed my choice maker, but the same thing happened again and I thought, now I'm in this part of the world, I'm in Thailand, and how many times will I ever be here again? What should I do? Well, maybe I *should* go to China, was the first thing that came to mind. And I pictured myself hitchhiking through China. Then I thought, no, I'd maybe get stuck on some tour of the cities and it would be hot and it would be crowded—maybe Nepal. I would get up there in the mountains—then I thought, too landlocked, down to Bali, maybe. So I had a kind of China-Nepal-Bali triangle going in my mind, and I would keep taking my ticket to the woman who was in charge of transportation on the film, and I would say, "Barbara, I think I'm going to be going to China."

"Well, Spalding," she'd say, "I think you've got to go

get a visa, and—why don't you just take the ticket? If you have trouble making up your mind, you deal with it. You've come to us enough."

Around about that time, while I was going through the different triangles, I went to the Art Department video viewing room in the hotel (where we could do all of our homework, see *Cambodia Year Zero* or any other videotapes about Cambodia we wanted to see), and watched a videotape called *Going Back*. It's about four veterans who go back to Hanoi on Christmas of 1981. They had been over originally to kill people, and now they were going back to make friends. . . . This was a fascinating tape. Tom Bird was one of the veterans in it, and he was also acting in *The Killing Fields*.

Now, I was really taken by the tape, not so much by the Amerasian children in the streets, although they were beautiful, or the people who were suffering in the hospitals from the effects of Agent Orange, but I was taken by the fact that Hanoi was filled with bicycles. I had never seen a city like it. The only sound to be heard was the sound of wind through bicycle spokes. And I thought, now there's where I'd like to go for my vacation. At least I wouldn't be a tourist there.

And I was beginning to feel more and more like "The Little Drummer Girl." I really wanted to be a *real* foreign correspondent, not someone *playing* one.

So I went to Tom Bird and asked, "What are our chances of going to Vietnam?" And he said, "We could will it. We could do it! We could do it if we put our minds to it. The best thing, Spalding, is to start off by going down to the Vietnamese embassy."

Now, I had been to the American embassy and I was very intimidated by it, because the air conditioning was so central that I couldn't tell where the cooling was coming from. There was no draft, it was just like sitting in this big cool glass block with beautiful flame trees outside the window. The Vietnamese embassy was not so modern. It was just down the road, but in contrast to the American embassy it was a lot like a very clean Polish men's room. It was very sparse and very simple—there was no furniture. Well, the only piece of furniture was in the main room and it was this beautiful teak table that we all sat around to talk with the embassy official. This table was exquisite. They must have rescued it from the bombing. On the surface there was a hand-carved, three-dimensional relief of elephants tearing down teak trees with their trunks in order to make the table—so, you see, it was a reflective table—it told a story about itself. In fact, it was doubly reflective, even *reflexive*, because it had a piece of glass over it and every so often I would catch a reflection of myself in the glass. I was wearing a blue cotton Thai peasant outfit from the Thai cottage industries, and the embassy official said, "They will like you very much in Hanoi with that outfit on."

The Vietnamese official really listened to us, whereas the American ambassador had kind of pontificated. This Vietnamese official was really curious about what Tom Bird and I wanted to do in Vietnam, and he asked us to write a letter to Hanoi laying out our proposal. He said, "First, before we begin our talk, could you please tell me—I've heard now that America has Vietnam on 'back burner.' Could you translate what means this 'back burner,' hm? Are we burning up?"

Tom, who is very politic, answered, "No—no. Look at it this way. Now, say you have some rice and you have some coffee. You guys are the rice and Central America is the coffee. And what we're doing is we're talking about putting the rice on the back burner to keep it warm because we want to heat up the coffee on the front."

"Ah, I see. Well, thank you very much. That explains that."

Then Tom said, "Now I would like you to meet America's number one Autobiographic Storyteller, Mr. Spalding Gray."

"Ah. Very pleased to meet you. Have you been on TV?"

I didn't know which way to go with this one. I didn't want to tell him right off that I didn't even *own* a television, particularly since I'd heard that NBC, CBS and ABC were going to be reporting from the streets of Hanoi come spring (providing that they'd agree to leave all their satellite equipment behind for the Vietnamese). And I was sure the Vietnamese wanted the American public at large to know certain things about Vietnam. So I thought, well, maybe I'd better go with it. I said, "I'm not on TV yet, but I've got it on the back burner, actually."

The David Letterman Show is interested. Every so often Jerry Mulligan, one of David's reps (and the son of an Irish cop from Cranston, Rhode Island), calls me up to find out how I'm doing: "David wants to know what's going on with that funny guy behind the table down-town. And he wants to know, Spalding, if you could *say something funny to me over the phone.*"

"What was that?"

"David wants you to *say something funny over the phone to me right now,* so I can tell it to him."

So I've got it on the back burner.

So, we decided that if it worked out, we would go to Vietnam. And I was able to reassure Renée, through Tom (Tom did it actually).

He just went to Renée and said in his deep, confident, assertive voice, "Renée, Spalding and I are going to Hanoi together and I will have him back in Krummville by July 8." And Renée said to me, "Why can't you talk like that? Take a lesson from Tom. Even if you don't mean it, at least you could say it and put me at ease. I mean, I've got a twenty-four hour flight ahead of me. It would be nice to go home with some sense of when I'll see you again. Write me a letter later but give me a break now, please."

Renée and I made up and we said a fond farewell out-side the gates of the Pleasure Prison. I'd made up my mind to stay with Tom. After all, maybe Thailand would be the right place to have a Perfect Moment. I had heard that the next location was in Phuket, where they had a lot of magic mushrooms, so if I didn't have an *organic* Perfect Moment, I could always induce one. Why not? And I would use Tom Bird as my Magic Will Carpet. I would leave as soon as he left, and we would either go to Vietnam or fly home together. He had a few more scenes in the film but I was finished. I had finished my last big scene of sixty-six takes, and now I was going to hang on until Tom finished his last scene. So I asked if I could travel with the company down to Phuket, which is this beautiful island in the Indian Ocean, off the southern coast of Thailand. They were going to film location shots at a Coca-Cola factory there, where Sidney Schanberg was supposed to have first seen the Khmer Rouge. (Actually, he first saw them at a Pepsi factory on the outskirts of Phnom Penh, but they couldn't find a Pepsi factory in Phuket, so they settled for Coke.)

Transportation told me that I could come along, but that I couldn't have my own driver anymore; I could go on the "Artists' Bus."

I got on the bus early in the morning. It was supposed to be a fifteen-hour trip, and we were told that *maybe* we would be stopped by bandits or Thai police. It would be more likely that the Thai army would rob us. The only road to Phuket was a dirt road, a *dirt road* through this jungle.

When I got on the bus I didn't see any Artists, so I wasn't really sure whether I was on the right bus or not. But there was an interesting bunch of people I'd never been with before. Uberto Pasolini of the Pasolini film-and-banking family from Rome: twenty-eight years old and had dropped out of the family business to carry orangeade for the film. He wanted to work his way up from the bottom and eventually become a film producer. He was sitting in the very front seat of this kind of old, '50s Greyhound bus; sitting in the very front seat, looking out, pretending his head was a camera and doing pans with his eyes of this meaningless jungle. He was happy.

Next to him were the Cambodian refugees from Long Beach. They had been hired to come along to be authentic reference points. If there were any questions to be asked about the authenticity of the film's locations, they could be asked. And since Pol Pot had killed all Cambodian actors, they had to play some of the roles, too, although they weren't actors; they weren't trained in any way. They were refugee social workers from Long Beach.

Then there was Neevy Pal, a Cambodian who was related to Prince Sihanouk and a student at Whittier College. Neevy was sitting in front of me and trying to organize all of the Cambodians in the bus because she felt *The Killing Fields* was a neo-colonialist film, that the British were looking right through the Cambodians. They were polite to the Americans and to each other, but they looked right through the Cambodians and treated them like refugees. So she was pissed, and she was trying to organize all the Cambodians into a sort of Consciousness-Raising Group.

Just to my right was this guy who was, I believe, an electrician—a Spark—or one of the cooks, and he was saying, "Spalding, what are you doing on this bus? Where's your driver? I would complain to British Equity if I were you." Meanwhile, there was a battle going on over the air conditioner. One minute it was up and the next it was down, and it was cold up front and warm in the back. He kept saying, "I would complain to British Equity if I were you. Where's your driver, boy? Where's your driver?"

And I said, "I'll tell you the truth, I'm not in the film anymore—"

"Oh, along for a freebee, are you? Oh, that's good work if you can get it. Well, that's good work then, isn't it?"

So, I was there feeling a little bit like I was in—Vermont, because the air conditioner was on so high. I had my raincoat on and my scarf wrapped around my neck. It was 110 degrees out, monsoon whipping down through those meaningless palms, and about seven hours into the trip we stopped for lunch.

I think it must have been the only restaurant on that entire road to Phuket and by the time we arrived all the actors, who had come in their private cars, had filled up the main dining room so I sat outside with all the Cambodian refugees from Long Beach. I ordered baked fish and just as it arrived a monsoon came up so fast that it just swamped my fish before I could get it under cover. I just left it and ran inside where I tried to order a fish to go.

After the monsoon passed I found myself standing, slightly soggy, by the Artists' Bus and there was Ivan (Devil in My Ear) in the parking lot, and he came up, looking a little Mephisphelean (he had a gray beard, handsome man), and he said, "Spalding. I'll be damned if I'm going to ride the rest of this next seven hours without being stoned. Will you join me in some Thai stick?"

I said, "Umm, all right, you know, I'll give it a try, um, since I haven't been drinking or arguing with Renée, all right, I'll do it."

So we took (puff-puff) just a couple of (puff) tokes

and I had this mild paranoia come over me, just *mild*. I said, "Ivan, by the way, what are you doing on the Artists' Bus? I notice that you're on it, too."

"I don't know how I got on it," he said. "I didn't even know they were calling it the Artist's Bus."

And I suddenly had a paranoid flash that there was *another* bus that we were supposed to be on, a much better bus, a perfectly air-conditioned Trailways bus gliding over a smooth macadam highway, filled with every kind of artist: Philip Glass, Laurie Anderson, John Lurie, Bill Irwin, Eric Bogosian, David Byrne, *Whoopi Goldberg.*

They were all there—with hookahs—talking interesting talk and lounging on these very comfortable mattresses and—worst of all—they were laughing! But then I just let all that go. I knew that it was just fantasy, just silly-billy paranoia and I thought, come on Spalding, either you're on the bus or you're off the bus. Be Here Now. And I found that I was on the bus and it was the right bus, the only bus and it was timeless, and I could have been in Thailand or Vermont. Inside, because of the air conditioner, it was like Vermont, and I put on my raincoat and wrapped my scarf around my neck and got out my little flask of Irish whiskey. Outside, it was like Thailand. In fact, it was Thailand. It was hot and the monsoon whipped down through meaningless palms like no travel poster I'd seen anywhere and it all looked like a Wallace Stevens poem:

A gold-feathered bird
Sings in the palm, without human meaning,
Without human feeling, a foreign song.

Inside the bus, Ivan had loaned me his stereo Walkman and I was finally catching up with Beethoven's String Quartets in Thailand. And looking out the window, monsoon pouring down, all of a sudden—in some timeless moment in the middle of the trip—we rounded this corner and there it was, this incredible vista of the Indian Ocean. I was totally not expecting it, I didn't expect it so soon or so late or so . . . I just didn't expect it.

It was like an oriental Hudson River School painting. The ocean was crashing in, this great white surf, the largest waves I had ever seen, under great, black monsoon skies, white birds blowing sideways, rainbows arching, palm trees ripping, Oh My God!—almost. About a number nine on my scale of ten for Perfect Moments. Had I been out there in my ocean briefs, I would have had to go home that afternoon.

Shortly after that we arrived at the Phuket Merlin, and it was so tacky, the rattiest hotel we'd been in. It wasn't near the water at all. I came into the hotel—we had been traveling for about fourteen hours—and out came this guy working on the film crew, a Thai, and he had this bucket filled with what looked like a mound of phosphorescent fungus glowing blue. And he said, "I've got them. I've got them. I've got all the magic mushrooms, all anyone needs."

Just *blooming* blue, they were *glowing* blue, these incredible magic mushrooms just giving off an aura of blue. I thought, there's no way I will take any substance from a man who smiles so much. He made me paranoid, he was so happy. It should be against the law, all that happiness—it was shocking. I was afraid that if I ate those mushrooms I'd never come back. That I'd end up staying on as a happy schoolteacher in Thailand.

The next day was a day off. I was staying with Tom Bird because I was trying to save all my money. I had $600 in Thai *bhat* saved up and I figured that if I didn't have a Perfect Moment, I would buy one. So I was staying in Tom's room, we were sharing a room, and on our day off some of us went down to what we had heard was Shangri-La—this most incredible beach.

Now I had thought this was just tourist hype. Every time I've traveled to foreign lands, I've always heard that Shangri-La was just around the corner. So we rented a car and we wound down through the water buffalo and the rice paddies and we came out on this *exquisite* beach. Ooh. No tourists. No flotsam. No jetsam. No cans. No plastic bags. Just water buffalo posing like statues in the mist at the far end of the beach. They were just standing there like they were stuffed. They looked like the Thai entry in the Robert Wilson Olympic Arts event. No ships out there in the Indian Ocean, huge surf—perfect Kodachrome day. The sun hadn't quite broken out and it was bright but not too sunny.

In the distance were some thatched huts where you could go have a little brunch and everyone went over there to order their fresh fish and pineapple and beer, and Ivan and I—like two kids—charged right down into the water. I couldn't believe it, it was body temperature, not too warm, just perfect. You could stay in it all day if you wanted to. I was charging in and out. Ivan went right out, right into the big stuff, but I stayed close to shore.

I was a little nervous about sharks. I have a lot of fears, phobias, and sharks and bears are at the top of the list. In fact, I'm the kind of guy who even checks out swimming pools before I go in. I often think some joker has put a shark in the pool as a practical joke. Also, I still had all my money tucked in my ocean briefs and I couldn't think of a good place to stash it. So I asked Ivan where I should put it and he said, "Oh, just leave it up on the beach where my cameras are."

He was a bit of a sadist playing into my masochism, and just as I was about to go into the water he said, "You know, in Africa when I put my cameras on the beach, the natives would just run right out of the jungle and take them. What are you going to do? Chase them into the jungle. Noooooo."

I was looking back at my money and coming and going, and then he said, "Well Spalding, Spalding, listen man. On our next day off I'm going to teach you how to scuba dive. You'll see fish you've never seen before, you'll have Rapture of the Deep, man, and it will be incredible."

And I said, "Oh my God, at last. It's like an initiation. I'll become a man." I've always wanted to overcome my fears with another guy, you know, skin diving and all that. I've always wanted to try scuba diving but I was afraid of sharks coming up from behind. And now Ivan would help me through my fears and become my scuba-guru.

Ivan said, "We'll go. And Spalding, you will see fish of all colors—you have never seen anything like it . . .

but there are these *Stone Fish* . . . and you don't want
to step on one of them Spalding, because you'll be dead
in seven seconds. There's no remedy, so wear your
sneakers."

He reminded me of when I was a kid with Kenny Ma-
son. Once when I was sledding in Barrington, Rhode
Island, Kenny said, "There's lions in those woods." I
was seven years old and I believed him. In Barrington,
Rhode Island, lions in winter. I ran all the way home,
crying.

So I was feeling like that seven-year-old again and I was
running in and out of the water like this excited kid
because I couldn't believe that I was there in Paradise
with Ivan. I didn't think I deserved to be in such a
beautiful spot and I'd run out of the water and down
the beach to try to get an overview. I'd run down the
beach and look back to try to see us there in the surf
and each time I'd miss myself and then run back to try
to be in it all again. Then down the beach and back
and down the beach and back and the third time back . . .
Ivan was gone. He had been out in the big surf and he
was *gone*, and I thought, oh no, holy shit. He's drowned.
Ivan has drowned.

I mean, these things do happen, people do drown. I've
read about it, and I read this warning issued by the film
which said, "Don't swim in Phuket." There had been
a number of drownings in recent years from the strong
undertow, and the very first thing that went through
my head—and it went very fast, the whole thing went

very fast—was, of course. He's drowned. Making a film about this much death, some real person actually has to go.

The next thing that went through my head was, it's not my fault! He was suicidal!

And the next thing was, quickly! Find the most responsible man you can. There was no way I was going to swim out in that water, I couldn't get out into that big surf. The first person that came to mind was John Swain, the Paris correspondent for *The London Times*. He had been there when the Khmer Rouge invaded Phnom Penh. He was perhaps the most narcissistic of the reporters, because he had come to Thailand to watch himself be played by Julian Sands. And so I just did it. I just screamed, "JOHN! JOHN SWAIN! COME QUICKLY, I CAN'T SEE IVAN!"

And everyone dropped their chopsticks and began to run. Some came across the swamp, some ran over the wooden bridge, and the first person to reach the beach was Judy Arthur, the publicist. Judy had been a lifeguard so she had the good sense to run along the high part of the beach. I was down by the dip of the lip of the sea and couldn't see out, and the others were trying to calm me down. My knees were shaking and I was on the verge of throwing up and people were saying, "Listen, Spalding. Take it easy. Take it easy. He won't drown, he's from South Africa." I was walking up and down the beach trying to interpret this, trying to figure it out, when Judy Arthur spotted Ivan way out. He had drifted down. Judy saw his head way out there and she called him in.

And I said, "My God, Ivan! Ivan, listen man, I thought you'd drowned. I really did."

He said, "Spalding, I'm really sorry, man. Listen, don't worry about me, I won't drown. I'm from South Africa."

Then everyone went back to brunch and I said, "Ivan, don't do that again, please." After promising he wouldn't, he turned to me and said, "By the way Spalding, when you called, how many came? Did Judy Freeman come?"

And I said, "Yes, Judy Freeman came, Judy Arthur came, all the Judies came. Let's go get something to eat."

So we walked over to brunch and suddenly I realized that I was with all these Real People, and I was feeling more and more like "The Little Drummer Girl." I was with these real foreign correspondents. Up until then I'd been hanging out with actors—they're no one. They're conduits. They're not as threatening as Real People. It's one thing to build a role from a text, just build it and develop it. It's another to be playing someone—you know—playing Mark Twain or Harry Truman all the way across the United States, and never *being* them.

But Mark Twain and Harry Truman are dead. And I was playing a guy who was alive. He works for the American embassy in Bangkok and he's a Princeton graduate and speaks six languages including Khmer. I graduated from Emerson College and am still wrestling with American. And these people are all like foreign correspondents, people who can just get on a plane and *go* with no sense of loss. One minute they're in Beirut, the next they're in a nuclear submarine off the coast of southern France, now they're here, eating and talking about their experiences. They see the whole world as their stage.

John Swain, for instance, was arguing with people about whether or not there's any cocaine in the Khyber

Pass. They were having an enormous discussion over that. Then Judy Arthur started talking about her sixth trip to China. Chris Menges, the cinematographer, was talking about his film, a trilogy he'd made tracing opium from Burma to Harlem. And he said there was a price on his head in Burma; the opium warlords who run the place wanted to kill him because he was with the good guys, and he had eighteen months of rushes on the back of a donkey that he couldn't get out of Burma. He was talking about that. Then there was Ivan, talking about how primitive the Amazon is. He was down there making a film about cocaine.

"Spalding, man! You should just go down there. It's unbelievable. It's truly wild. No Buddhist inhibitions, like here in Thailand."

Then there was Roland Neveu, who had just flown in after photographing Beirut. He had been in Phnom Penh when the Khmer Rouge came in, and now he was here testing out his new underwater camera—just dropped in to say, "Hi ho mates," and have a beer before heading for a nuclear submarine off the coast of southern France.

And there was Minty Clinch, a publicist, who was talking about hitchhiking through Patagonia. Skip the hitchhiking; I couldn't even visualize Patagonia. And there was this beautiful woman who was on a forty-day fast. She was half Thai and half Scottish. What a mix. Oh, la-la.

Her mother had come over from Scotland to marry a Thai man—just the opposite of the way it usually is. They were both doctors, and they had this baby who turned into this fasting woman. She had these almond eyes, these Thai eyes and this Thai complexion, but this WASPish-Anglican bone structure and freckles, and she was very beautiful.

She was there fasting for forty days. She had first learned to fast at a Texas fast farm, and now she was here in Thailand doing it on her own, while watching us eat.

And then there was me, who was looking at this incredible bee that looked like a cartoon of a bee because it was so big and fluffy, and its stripes were so wide, and I was saying, "Wow! Look at that bee."

And everyone said, "It's just a bee, Spalding."

Soon, lunch was over and it was time to go back in swimming. Ivan and I rushed down to the beach like the two kids who couldn't wait an hour after eating.

And Ivan said, "Hey, let's toke up."

I said, "All right. God knows I can let my Kundalini out on this beach." It used to get stuck in my lower Chakra, but I knew I could just run it off on the beach.

I took two tokes and had a mildly paranoid episode about my money and where to hide it. At first I started digging holes in the sand, but then I changed my mind and went to hide it under the rubber mat in the van. Then I thought that this focus of all my concentration on hiding the money was setting up mind waves that could be read by the Thais and that they would find the money. And God knows they needed it more than I did. So, at last I just took it and left it, fully exposed, on the beach.

I could see Ivan way out in the big surf calling,

"Spalding! Spalding! I see you like the little waves. You don't know what living is until you get out here into this big stuff!" I really wanted to get out there.

I kept going out a little further and each time, I would think of my money being stolen and I was less afraid of sharks. It just sort of happened naturally. I realized I was out a little further and a little further until all of a sudden I was out further than I had ever been in any ocean, in any world, anywhere. I was beyond Ivan even. I was so far out—I could tell that I had never been in this situation before because of the view of the shoreline. I had never seen the shore from that point of view before. It was so far away that I felt this enormous disconnection from Mother Earth.

Suddenly, there was no time and there was no fear and there was no body to bite. There were no longer any outlines. It was just one big ocean. My body had blended with the ocean. And there was just this round, smiling-ear-to-ear pumpkin-head perceiver on top, bobbing up and down. And up the perceiver would go with the waves, then down it would go, and the waves would come up around the perceiver, and it could have been in the middle of the Indian Ocean, because it could see no land. And then the waves would take the perceiver up to where it could look down this great wall of water, to where Judy Arthur and John Swain were body surfing—like on a Hawaiian travel poster—far below, and then—"Whoop!" The perceiver would go up again. I don't know how long this went on. It was all very out of time until it was brought back into time by Ivan's voice calling, "Spalding! Spalding, come back, man! I haven't tested those waters yet!"

I believed him and I thought that I was in trouble.

And I fell back into time and back into my body and I swam in to Ivan. We treaded water together. I was panicked, always expecting to feel "Chomp!"—you know, just "Chomp!"—the whole lower part of my body gone from a big shark bite. Because now I was back in fearful time. I was also sad because I knew I'd had a Perfect Moment and I would now have to go home. And Ivan swam out to test my waters and he came back in choking . . .

"Oh-ahkkkhhh!"

. . . water pouring out of his nose and mouth and he said, "Spalding, man, now I know what it's like to drown. I almost drowned out there."

And I thought, oh, shit. Now *I'm* going to have to go out and "almost drown." No. No, I won't fall into this male competitive trap. I *know* what Ivan's idea of a Perfect Moment is. It's Death!

So I swam in and joined up with Penny Eyles, the Continuity lady. Just who I needed at that point

I said, "Penny, listen, I had a Perfect Moment but I have no words for it. But I can tell you about my new theory of Displacement of Anxiety. You see, if you ever want to do something Penny, and you're afraid to do it and you lack the courage, just take a big pile of money and leave it somewhere where it can be stolen. Then you'll be able to do what has to be done. Just concentrate on your money."

She said, "Spalding, Spalding, you're a strange bloke. You know what? You think too much. What are you doing testing your fears at forty-two years old? Didn't you do it as a lad?"

"No," I said. "Was I supposed to? Oh lord, did I miss that, too? Oh no, I know, my brother Rocky did it all for me. He tested all his fears at an early age. One of his biggest fears was the basement in our house. When our parents would go away he'd turn out the lights and crawl on his belly from his bedroom down the front stairs, then down the basement stairs and, with his eyes closed, he would feel the basement walls, every crack, feeling his way around the entire room until he either died or didn't die."

So Penny said, "I want you to walk with me down this beach without looking back once at your money. We will walk to the far end of the beach together. Let's go."

And I walked all the way down the beach with Penny backwards, never once losing sight of my money. Then, when I got down to the far end of the beach I fell into a new cluster of energy. There were these enormous water buffalo that came up to my shoulder and these ratty, ragtag Thai kids with sticks talking to the buffalo in Thai and ignoring me. I was floating in between this boy-buffalo energy like Casper the Friendly Ghost. I was in their energy field, in my ocean briefs and ready to go anywhere they went. I was being swept away, just like the water. I was going with them and I was happy, and all of a sudden a human voice woke me and I drowned as I heard, in the distance, Judy Freeman calling, "Spalding! Spalding! Time to go. Time to go back to the Phuket Merlin."

So I went. I had to. These people had become my umbilical cord. I was breathing through them.

I got back to the hotel and I went to the person who

was fast becoming my father-confessor, Athol Fugard. Now, Athol seemed to like hearing my stories, and also, he had just given up drinking so he was buying me drinks and kind of living vicariously through me.

"Spalding! I am going to have an orange and you will have yourself some beer. Now. What's been going on? Tell me all about your day."

And I told him. I told him about the Perfect Moment in the Indian Ocean and he said, "Spalding. The sea's a lovely lady." (He's South African, like Ivan.) "The sea's a lovely lady when you play in her, but if you play *with* her, she's a bitch. Don't ever play with the sea. You're lucky to be here. You're lucky to be alive."

I believed him, and we went to eat—Athol, Graham Kennedy, Tom Bird and I. Afterwards Tom and I went window-shopping for whores and then went to bed. I slept rocked in the arms of the sea, like a kid again in Jerusalem, Rhode Island with sand in my bed. It was a beautiful night, perfect sleep, the bed rocking gently.

The next day was June 24 and it was a back-to-work day for those that were still working on the film. I wanted to hang out on the set because it was supposed to be a very . . . explosive day, when the first bombs went off at the Coca-Cola factory.

When I got down to the set everything was in perpetual flames, like a little version of hell. All the buildings had flaming gas jets around them so they could burn all day without burning down. Coke trucks were burning as well, and I got to throw cases of Coke at the wall, to smash the bottles, make it look like a bomb had blown up. And the Thai extras were lined up, covered with chicken giblets, fake blood and what looked like very real third-degree burns created by the art department. They were all lined up and smiling. While we were trashing the area I decided that I wanted to talk to certain people. I had a sense that Tom might be through with his role in the film any time and we'd have to leave, either for Hanoi or Krummville. So I was going into that kind of state when you think you're about to die or leave a place forever, and you want to just get to know everyone before you go

Keith, the costumier, was first. I hadn't talked with him. He'd always struck me as a little mad, and I was telling him about my theory of Displacement of Anxiety and he said, "I know all about it. Oh, sure. I've got a witch up there, white one, up in Nottingham. Oh, she's a blessed one. Every time I fly she gets mildly ill, in a pub, you see? She gets sick. She takes on my anxiety and I have a lovely flight. I know all about it. I knew this actress. She hated a fellow actor and she wanted to get him out of the show. She stuck a note on the stairs, under the carpet on the stage. It said, 'May you trip and break your leg.' And he did. Oh, I know all about it."

Then I went on from Keith to talk to Haing Ngor. Now I hadn't talked directly to Haing about his story, but I certainly had heard about it. I think I felt ashamed, or I didn't want to bother him, because people had asked him about his story so many times before. He was playing the role of Dith Pran. Now, Haing had also been tortured for years under the Pol Pot regime, so to some extent he was reenacting his own life story as well as Pran's. As the story goes, Haing was a Cambodian gynecologist and he had been performing an emergency operation on someone in Phnom Penh when the Khmer Rouge broke into the hospital and demanded to know where the doctor was. Haing just threw down his stuff and said, "I'm not a doctor, I'm a taxicab driver. I drove the doctor here." And he left the patient on the operating table and became a cab driver from that day on.

The other thing about Haing Ngor that interested me was his anger. Of all the Cambodians that I met, his anger was most on the surface, and I think that's why he was cast in the role.

The others were always smiling. It was hard to believe they could still be smiling, but they were always smiling about everything. I don't know what it came from, the Buddhism or that they'd seen too much to talk about, but they were always very gentle and smiling. But Haing's rage was right there, and I went up and asked him what had happened to him.

"They put! Plastic! Plastic bag. Over my head!"

"And then?"

"And then. They take me. They tie me to a cross. And burn my legs. And burn me right here."

And he showed me the burn marks on his legs.

"They burned you? How did you get through this? What were you thinking about? What was going on?"

"I know. If I tell the truth. I'm one hundred percent dead. Now I'm only ninety-eight percent dead. The truth. Hundred percent dead."

"How did you escape?"

"They take me. And Khmer Rouge put. Me in jail."

"They put you in jail, yes, and . . ."

"They. Burn it down."

The Khmer Rouge were really crazy. They put him

in jail and then set fire to it and, of course, the prisoners ran out. Some got burned, yes. Some escaped. Haing escaped and ate his way across Cambodia on bark and bugs—the traditional diet—leaves and lizards. At last he made it to a Thai refugee camp and now he's living in L.A.

Then I went to the Sparks, the British electricians. I envied their sort of blissful ignorance the most. They were the ones who, as soon as they arrived in Thailand, went down and bought Thai wives. Now I think it's a class thing. None of the actors did it. The electricians could do it. I don't know if it has to do with electricity or what, but I know the actors didn't buy women out front. They were more secretive about it and would sneak around doing it at night. These guys went right out and got these women and they made a little laughing family. I used to listen at their hotel doors sometimes. They'd be in there speaking pidgin English to each other in the shower.

"Hey, beeg guy, ohkeekyouass I keeckassoh ho ho ho!" laughing. I mean the major English they knew came from the popular records there: "Lies, Lies, Lies, Liar," and "Do You Want to Funk?" During the day the Thai wives hung out by the pool together and talked, and at night the men came home from work and everyone went out to eat. The Thai women knew just what to order and everyone had a good time there, laughing. The women talked among themselves and the men talked among themselves—now, not a radical idea, granted, but a lot happier than most nuclear families that I've come across in any McDonald's or Howard

Johnson's. A lot more laughter coming off the table. I don't know what laughter is indicative of, but it has something to do with joy and letting go.

I've been with prostitutes in Amsterdam and New York City, and they are very cool, business-as-usual. It's like going to a very cold doctor. You just wouldn't naturally fall in love with one. But I think that you could very easily fall in love with a Thai whore, very easily. They really seemed to be having a good time there, feeding coconut-flavored rice to the Sparks as they lounged before them like gargantuan Gauguins. If, in fact, they were all acting, then a good many of them should have received Academy Awards along with Haing Ngor.

And yes, I've heard the other side of it and I know it exists the way the darker side of everything exists. Just recently, while driving in L.A., I heard a very angry woman talking on KPFK Radio about an investigation she had made of child prostitution in Thailand. She said that evil people were kidnapping ten-year-old girls and bringing them to the city to be prostitutes, and they were chaining them to the beds like slaves. When one of the whorehouses burned down all they found were these charred ten-year-old skeletons, chained to beds. I didn't hear about this until after I got back from Thailand, but while I was there it all looked like fun. I wanted in on it all, but I couldn't get in because I was too conflicted.

Then, all of a sudden, the guns went off and the machine-gun fire started, and the bombs. Five hundred Coke cases were blown across the warehouse. John Swain was running off camera behind Julian Sands, who was playing him, and John was yelling, "What a lovely war!

What a great war! You know you're not going to get shot!'' This confirmed my whole idea of War Therapy.

We were running through the machine-gun fire, the black smoke pouring off burning rubber tires, and all of a sudden it was lunchtime. We all sat down at a table with these Thai peasants who were completely covered with blood—it looked like their faces were falling off— and we were all eating together when a monsoon suddenly came up and one of the tents blew down and a real Thai woman got knocked out for real. They carried her in and put her in the middle of the table where the food was. So it was the monsoon versus the film. Then the monsoon passed and the film began again and there was so much black smoke you couldn't even see the sky. There were rockets and machine-gun fire, and Judy Freeman, who was on sound, said to me, ''Spalding, my God, what are you feeling guilty about? What are you doing in the middle of a war when you could be down on Paradise Beach? Chris and I have rented a house down there that we never use. You're free to use it. Go, go. Have fun.''

So I thought, ooh, why not? What am I feeling guilty about? After all, let's not waste time on that.

I walked out—it was incredible. What a beautiful day. The sun was out, I felt like I was in seventh grade and I was just walking out of school at ten in the morning. Just a free boy. And I went back to the hotel and got Billy Paterson and his girlfriend Hildegarde and some of the Cambodian refugees, and we hired a car and went back to Karon Beach. Now, it wasn't as beautiful this time, it never is the second time around, but it was beautiful. And I was walking down the beach—completely empty, beautiful day, big surf—with one of the Cambodian refugees, and I said, "So, what are you doing here? I mean what have you been doing—aren't you getting bored?"

"No, I'm 'fighting' every night. Last night I 'fought' six times."

"What do you mean, 'fighting'?"

It turned out that this was a euphemism for fucking. For some reason the Cambodians had all these code words for their amorous escapades. If a Cambodian was going for a massage, he'd refer to it as "going for an interview." This particular code had grown out of the fact that one of the Cambodians was there with his wife, and every time he went out for a massage and she asked where he was going, he told her he was going to be interviewed about the movie. (He had a very small role.)

So, massage equaled "interview" and fucking equaled "fighting."

"You 'fought' six times last night?" I said. "Aren't you afraid of that new Southeast Asian strain of gonorrhea that's supposed to be so strong that it's knocking down doors?"

"No, no. Haing is a Cambodian gynecologist. He told me what to do. He says after you 'fight' you drink a lot of beer to wash out the germs and in the morning you eat a lot of penicillin."

So he was on a beer/penicillin diet. And he believed in it. He claimed it was working. We walked on the beach and he picked three fresh coconuts for us. He cut the tops off and we were drinking fresh coconut milk when we came upon two tourists. Now, on a beach like that, if you come upon only two tourists, sure, you're going to stop and talk.

It was Jack and Mary from Saudi Arabia—Mary via Dublin and Jack via Washington State. Mary was a nurse in Saudi Arabia and Jack was a plastic surgeon. They were traveling companions. They'd come on a vacation but Jack was particularly interested in Thailand because he said there were challenges in the plastic surgery field like in no other country. Jack had heard about the jealous Thai wives who cut off men's cocks and feed them to the ducks. And he had heard about the special plastic surgery wings where doctors sewed them back on. He said there were more challenges in plastic surgery in Thailand and the Philippines than in any other country, so he was thinking of staying on.

"Come! Come join us for lunch," I cried. "Come sup with us—tell us of your travels of the world." It was all like a big Hemingway novel. "Come! Sit! Tell us about Saudi Arabia!"

Mary started: "Well, Saudi Arabia, my God. Man, you would not believe how primitive it is. They still have public executions there, and if you're a foreigner you just get pushed right up to the front and when you see the head come off, plop, you faint dead away. Oh, and they cut off hands there. They cut off hands for thievery and they cauterize the stumps in boiling oil. Oh, also, they still do stoning, oh, do they ever. And it's modern. It's a more contempoary style—I was there. There was this woman, she was an adulteress and she got pregnant. They waited for the baby to be born, then they buried her in sand up to her neck and drove a big dump truck up filled with stones and just dumped them on her head. That's their modern stoning method. What do you think of that?"

I said, "Good God! Thank God I live in America!"

So the conversation ran its course and spiraled down, as it often does at any dinner table, from sex, death and taxes to shit and money, depending on whether it's mixed company. In this case it was mixed company, so it all ended with money. Now I don't mind talking about money. When people ask me what I make, I tell them. But for many, money is a taboo subject. My father would never talk about it. He never told how much he made.

It all started when Billy Paterson said to me, "So Spalding, what are you going to do with all the money you make?"

"What? What money?" This was a medium-budget film, about twenty million, and I had been told that everyone was making the same salary except Sam Waterston who was making a little more, and the Cambodians who were making a lot less.

And Billy said, "Well, I'll tell you if you tell me."

"All right. You go first."

"Well, as far as I know all the Brits are making $3,000 a week plus $325 a week for expenses."

"Ohuhoh. I thought I was doing very well, but I'm making $1,500 plus $325, and $3,000 is twice as much, isn't it?"

"Well, Spalding, you know, maybe that's because you don't have an agent."

All of a sudden I saw white. Of course! An agent! What am I doing lying on the beach like an old hippie at forty-two years old, trying to have Perfect Moments in Thailand? What am I doing searching for Cosmic Consciousness? Cosmic Consciousness belongs to the independently wealthy in this day and age. Go! Get an agent! Yes! Do not go to Hanoi! Do not pass Go! Go directly to Hollywood and get an agent! After all, what is this film about? Survival! Whose survival? My survival. Go! Get an agent! Go do five Hollywood films you don't really like. Do them! Get a house out in the Hamptons where you can have your *own* Perfect Moments in your *own* backyard. Have your friends come over for an afternoon of Perfect Moments. Return to your own ocean. Go! Go! Go to Hollywood and get an agent!

Exhausted from this epiphany, I staggered down to the beach, and went into a semi-miasma sleep in which I thought I was back on Long Island, in the Hamptons, hearing the sound of my own ocean without ever having to travel twenty-four hours on Thai Air. And I was half asleep when I heard someone yelling, "Boat People! Boatpeopleboatpeopleboatpeople *Boat People!*"

I woke to see the Thai waiter from the restaurant looking out to sea with binoculars and I got up and looked out. And, way out, I saw this ancient old craft like an old wooden cider tub, bobbing with all these little heads along the edge like Wynken, Blynken and Nod. They were *way* out there and some Thai fishermen were trying to lasso their boat, and they looked like real Vietnamese boat people. But was it the real thing? I couldn't believe it—just when I was beginning to forget about Vietnam and dream of the Hamptons, these wretched sea gypsies came into view.

And Jack—Jack from Saudi Arabia via Washington; Jack who was the kind of guy who was so in touch with his body he was out of touch with it; the kind of guy who would climb Mount Everest for the weekend just to ski down it and videotape himself doing it—Jack walked over, pulled down his goggles and proceeded to go in the water, like in a cartoon.

And like a buzz saw he cut right through my Perfect Moment area . . .

right through Ivan's chartered waters . . .

and disappeared into the Indian Ocean.

I was pacing up and down the beach. Twenty minutes later he strolled back out of the ocean and I said, "What the fuck? Where were you? Where'd you go?"

And he said, in that casual, laid-back, almost indifferent way, "Oh, I just wanted to swim out and see if they were real boat people, but they got towed away before I got out there."

"Jack, how far out would you say that was?"

"Oh, a mile, mile-and-a-half."

"Do you do that sort of thing often?"

"Well, I do like long distance swimming. Once, when I was swimming about two-and-a-half hours off the coast of Jersey . . ."

"Two-and-a-half hours? What if a thunderstorm had come up?"

A distant, whimsical smile passed as Jack said, "Yeah . . . I ran into this big leviathan-type thing, I mean whatever it was, it should not have let me hit it, and I panicked and started to swim in."

(If you can imagine the quality of a panicked swim two-and-a-half hours out.)

"I swam in and the next day a guy had his leg bitten

off right to his knee, in knee-deep water, by a shark. So I just might have run into that shark but I was lucky and hit it in the nose."

Jack and Mary wanted to ride into town with us. They said Shangri-La was not very interesting at night. In fact, it was a bore and all they did was "fight." They wanted to dine with us in town.

"Sure. C'mon in. There's always interesting configurations—there are 130 of us. Sometimes you eat meals with people you like, other times you just go along and discover new people.

When I got back to the hotel I found that Tom Bird had finished his last scene and I thought, oh, God, time for the Last Supper. So I was really kind of down and I tried to talk Tom into staying on for a few days and going to Karon Beach.

"Tom, you've got to stay. You've really got to stay. We're going to have a beautiful, beautiful time at the beach, take the magic mushrooms. Just stay about three extra days?"

"Spalding, brush that sand off your legs before you come in here."

So I knew something weird was going on. I really should have confronted him on it. If I have any major regrets about this trip, it was that I didn't confront Tom Bird about why he wouldn't go to that beach.

It was time for dinner and a bunch of us went to an outdoor restaurant right on the edge of the Indian Ocean. There were about twenty of us and it all looked and felt like a big Thanksgiving dinner, the Last Supper right at the edge of the world. The islands beyond, over

which sweet, cooling trade winds blew, gave off no light
or life. It was just us and the Thai waiters moving under
multicolored Japanese lanterns that swayed in the winds.

David Puttnam sat at the head of the table and I sat
to his left with my back to the sea. David was holding
up a picture of John Malkovich and saying, "So, I hear
John doesn't want to do any more films. He says he
wants to return to the Steppenwolf Theatre Company
in Chicago." John was sitting at the far end of the table
and I was a little drunk and saying, "Yes, I think the
lady doth protheth too much." John was winking back
at me and taking it all good-naturedly.

Now, I was feeling a little competitive, I admit it. I
had been doing solo performance for so long that I had
forgotten all that competitive stuff that comes up when
you begin to mix and mingle with a lot of Talent. I had
been down at the Performing Garage for so long that
I'd lost touch with that scene. I know that not only is
John a good actor, he's also a good storyteller. He could
be sitting behind a table just like I do somewhere far
away, let's say in Chicago or Alaska, telling stories not
unlike these.

My question is, could I play Biff on Broadway? Are
we interchangeable? John just gets work. It seems to
just come to him because he's not needy. Also, he has
a good manager. It's not just that he has an agent, he
also has a *very good* manager. In fact, I don't know if
you noticed, but when *The Killing Fields* was reviewed
in *The New York Times*, there was also a small article
in another part of the paper about the blackout on the
Q.E. II, and who did they contact to interview by telephone satellite? John Malkovich. How did he get on
the Q.E. II? His manager. And how did *The Times* know

he was there? His manager. And how did the lights go out? His manager. (And how did Ronald Reagan become President?) They set it up like that to get the reverb. It's an echo—you see, the review isn't enough.

Now, I'm sitting at the table and it's not that John Malkovich reminds me of my brother, or that David Puttnam reminds me of my father, but there is some archetypal family scene going on there. I mean, like David Puttnam, my father sat at the head of the table, but he never talked as much as David Puttnam. The only two things my father ever said were, "All things are relative" and "Whatever you do, marry a wealthy woman." Now I thought that was good advice. You had the physical and the metaphysical. And he was a good provider, like David Puttnam.

Every Sunday there was steak and every Monday there was a roast—roast beef, roast lamb. And I can remember on Monday, passing my plate up for more of that blood-rare roast beef. I wasn't hungry, you know, but I was going up for thirds. Now, I know to some extent I was trying to eat my father's body. I understand that. But I would pass it up anyway, and he would send it back and it would have to go by my brother Rocky—Rockwell Junior, who was kind of the autocrat of the table. He would take a big piece of beef off my plate and pop it into his mouth. And I would say, "What was that about?" and he'd say, "Toll."

Also, Rocky had a game called "Dime." He had a paper route and so he often had a pocket full of dimes, and he would run around yelling "Dime!" and if you touched him, you got a dime. But just before you touched him he'd say, "Deal's off!" He also had a proclamation of "Forbidden Names." The names that rubbed him the wrong way all just happened to be my friends' names, and if I said them, I got hit. No big deal. The names were nothing special—I mean, I look both ways before I say them now, actually.

"Lucille Bisbano . . ." (Pow!)

"Steve Sea . . ." (Punch! Punch!)

"Heather Henry . . ." (Chop! Chop!)

Then my little brother Channing was born. When Chan was born I knew what jealousy was, because Rocky fell in love with Chan. And one warm summer day when he was four years old, I led Chan naked into the middle of Rumstick Road and stood him on the white line and told him to stay there. My mother rushed out just in time to save him from the speeding cars.

Now, I'm not saying that Chan is John Malkovich, or that David Puttnam is my father—but there we were, and something of that family order was going down, and I was hoping David Puttnam would pay for the meal. (He didn't.) It was my Last Supper and I really wanted him to know. I wanted him to love me so much that he could read my mind. After all, he had paid for Craig T. Nelson's last meal. They had a huge party when Craig T. left, but Craig was a Professional Actor, and he left as soon as his last scene was over. If Craig didn't have another job to go to, at least he acted like he did, and I was beginning to feel like this poor relative.

The reason I know that John Malkovich is a good story-teller is that we had to tell dirty jokes. The film was a "buddy" movie, it was about *male bonding*. I'd never been with men in a situation like this in my life. I was never in a fraternity. I was never in any kind of male bonding situations. And we'd all get together for lunch, or cocktails at six, and we'd all just sit around and *bond*, talking about what happened that day.

And at one particular luncheon, a Cambodian refugee who wanted to bring back dirty jokes for his friends in Long Beach asked us to tell some for his collection. He asked people to go around in a circle and tell dirty jokes. I didn't know any dirty jokes—I couldn't think of any—but I wanted to be one of the guys so when my turn came I said, "All right, all right. There was this couple . . ." (I remembered one) "a generic couple, we'll call them Dick and Jane. It was back in the fifties. It was their first date and they were both very uptight. Dick was very nervous about his appearance there in Jane's living room, and there was a dog, too, Spot. Jane's dog, Spot, a collie asleep on the floor. So Dick had done everything to prepare himself: 5-Day Stay-Dry Deodorant Pads, Aqua-Velva, Listerine. Jane was the same, all scrubbed down with Lysol and properly dressed. They were just, you know, petting in the living room—except Dick was very nervous and he had gone off his diet. Just before coming over, he had eaten a big bowl of baked beans with red cabbage on top. And for dessert, he'd had two green pears and some figs and raisins. So he was letting out those Silent But Deadly, unbelievable steamy hot burners. You wouldn't hear them come but when they filled the room you *knew* it. He would just ease them out as he leaned over to kiss Jane on the cheek, and then as he leaned back, he'd say, 'Oh, Spot! Good God! Jane, where'd you get this dog? Did you say it was a thoroughbred collie?' And then Dick would ease out another one and say, 'Oh, Spot! Oh! One more like that and we'll take you to the pound to have you gassed on your own gas.' Then, just as Dick let loose with the last hot burner, Jane leapt up and yelled, 'C'mon Spot, let's get out of here before he shits on us both!' "

That was all I could think of. Oh, no, wait. There was one other. "This traveling salesman who is desperate to find a room stops at this hotel in the South and the owner says there aren't any more rooms. 'There's one upstairs but you can't have it.'

'Why?'

'Well, the screens are ripped, there are flies. You wouldn't sleep. There's every kind of fly. There's bottle flies, green flies, deer flies, black flies and house flies, and you wouldn't sleep, I'm telling you. Horse flies, even.'

'I'll take it.'

And the next morning, he comes down completely rested and the manager says, 'You look like you slept. What'd you do?'

'Just a little "bunching." I had to bunch the flies.'

'What do you mean, you "bunched" the flies?'

'Well, I took a shit in the corner and I went to bed!' "

So then it was John Malkovich's turn. And, by the way, the Cambodian was laughing at every line. I don't know if it had to do with the translation, the Buddhist Tolerance, the polymorphous perverse quality of the Cambodian culture or what. But the Cambodians, at least this one, didn't seem to have any concept of "punch line." The whole joke seemed to be funny to him, and he'd laugh at every line.

Anyway, it was John's turn and he said, "There was this elephant . . ."

"Hhha-ha-ha," the Cambodian is already laughing.

". . . and a mouse. And the mouse was in love with the elephant. And there was a monkey up in a tree throwing down coconuts, screaming monkey invectives. The elephant was a gal and the mouse was a guy, and the mouse was trying to mount the elephant. It was erotic love. And the mouse would take these little running jumps and bounce off the back of the elephant. At last, the mouse took a long run and made it up and just as it mounted the elephant, the monkey hit the elephant on the head with a coconut and the elephant fell to its knees, totally stunned. And the mouse cried out, 'Yeah! Suffer, bitch!' "

So I turned to the Cambodian and asked, "Which joke did you like?"

"Malkovich! The Malkovich joke!"

"All right, tell it back, 'cause I want to hear if you got the punch line."

"There was an elephant. Ahh-hah-hah. And a mouse, and the mouse was in love with the elephant. Eh-heh. And there was a monkey up in the tree. And the monkey yells down, 'HEY ELEPHANT! YOU MAKE GOOD LOVE!' "

So I was feeling a little on edge. It was my last night there and Mary, the nurse from Saudi Arabia via Dublin, was next to me and she was driving me nuts. She kept calling me "Baldwin"—"Baldwin" this, "Baldwin" that. I kept correcting her and she'd say, "Baldwin, you would not *believe*—you think the Saudis are stupid? Oh, my God man, the Pakistanis are even worse. I tell you, I was a nurse there and I had to get a urine sample from this Pakistani bloke. I gave him a little jar and he went behind a curtain and an emergency came up and I forgot about him. Two hours later he came out and handed me the bottle and it had a half-inch of sperm in it. And he said, 'That's all I could get in two hours.' "

Back at the hotel I fell asleep and I dreamt that I was taking care of some pet fish and I put them in the oven with some wild fish and forgot all about them, and then I thought, oh, my God, they're burning up. And I went and opened the oven and the fish were looking back at me with these intelligent, human eyes. And one of them turned into John Malkovich, who seemed completely indifferent to being saved.

The next day was my last, and I felt as if I were going to the gallows. I wanted to say goodbye like a man, and if I couldn't be one, I was going to imitate one. I had seen enough of them, been on the film, watched how everyone behaved. And I went around to each person and acted as though I'd made up my mind.

"Goodbye, mate."

"Yep, take it easy. I'll work with you again. You look out for those whores, now."

"Oh, yeah."

"Hey, big guy. It's been good workin' with you."

"Goodbye."

"Yeah."

"It's a beautiful film."

"Yeah, I really believe in it."

"Right, bye."

"Yeah."

"Hey, guys, it doesn't get much better than this."

And when I got to Athol Fugard, he turned to me and said, "So, Spalding. You're leaving Paradise?"

"Athol (oh!) Athol (I!) uh, Athol (uh!), I—I was thinking that maybe I should (oh!) eh, uh, wait a minute, Athol, you really think I, uh . . ."

"Return to Renée. She's a lovely lady. Go back, Spalding! Take what you've learned here and go back. It's all the same, you know."

I wanted to believe him.

And Tom and I got on the plane back to Bangkok. As soon as we arrived, Tom went right to the Vietnamese embassy and I went right to John Malkovich's tailor over on Silom Road and said, "You know that suit that John Malkovich had made here? The one that looked sort of sloppy and sort of neat all at once? The one that looked something like a cross between a suit and a parachute?"

"Oh, yes. He designed it himself."

"Make me one just like it."

"Surely Mr. Gray can afford two suits at such a price."

"All right, two—one brown and one gray—and three of the shirts, the Malkovich shirts. The ones he had copied from that Paris design."

I went back to the hotel, where Tom told me that we might have to wait three or four more days before we could get into Vietnam.

I said, "Well, what do you think?"

"No. I have to get back to Sis."

Tom's girlfriend's name was Sis and they had rented a house with some other people in Bridgehampton, Long Island for the summer. I realized then that I was riding on his Love/Libido Carpet. It was no longer the Magic Will Carpet. And I said, "Tom, couldn't you go with me tonight to Pat Pong and at least work out the sexual part of it? You know, we'll pick up some Thai gals and let off some of the pressure from the old pressure cooker?"

"No. I've got to get back. I went to those whores during the war and got gonorrhea twice. I'm not interested."

"Well, would you come down with me then so I can say goodbye to Joy?" Joy was my Pat Pong girlfriend.

Going down to the Captain's Table where Joy worked seemed like a kind of strange homecoming. Her whole face lit up when she saw me and she really seemed happy. We did what we'd always done the three or four times I'd visited her before. We sat in a corner of the bar and I put my arm around her and we watched the other girls dance until closing time. There was nothing to say. She didn't speak English and I didn't speak Thai. She sat there almost naked in her two-piece bathing suit. I had no idea how old she was. Maybe nineteen.

She had a perfectly exquisite body. It was very small and childlike but at the same time ripe and fully developed like that of a mature woman. She was a splendid, dark miniature and what I loved most was the texture of her skin. Joy was a joy to touch and knowing that I could, for a little extra money, go home with her at any time, I preferred that kind of suspended waiting and almost innocent touching.

She did her best to keep smiling whenever I looked

at her, but there were times when I was able to steal a secret glance and then I would see another side of Joy. I would catch her in a slightly drained and more reflective melancholy state, and I realized how much was always going on behind the scenes and how little I knew or wanted to know. Most of all I realized that I could never get to it without language.

It was then that I realized that I was just like all the others, a lonely displaced man in Thailand, and like all the others I couldn't live long without the simple touch of women. At first I'd seen them all around me on the streets and I was satisfied to live only in my eyes. To gaze on their flesh was enough. But after awhile I needed to touch and it was not unlike the way in which I needed to take my shoes off in order to dig my toes into Karon Beach.

You see, when you see that river of flesh coming at you in the streets, it's very hard not to want to touch. It's very hard not to see one flesh as all flesh. You get taken over like a curious child. At first Joy seemed happy to see me and we could ride on that novelty. The softness of her skin was like a kind of heaven on earth and I wanted to keep it that way and not think. But when I sat long enough with Joy I could see the joy drain out and a kind of melancholy despondency creep into her face. And when the stage lights went out and the house lights came up at quarter to one, I could see everyone scatter like cockroaches under fluorescent light. And I could see the bruises like rotten fruit on the girls' legs.

When we got back to the hotel I realized something was wrong—because two basic intentions in making love are pleasurable relief through sex, and some rec-

ognizable change in "the other." I could never really
see the change in this particular other. And why should
I expect change? After all, I was paying her. And I figured whatever she said or did was just an act. Also I
think it had a lot to do with language. Eighty percent
of erotic love for me is the language in and around the
event. But she spoke very little English. All she could
(or would) say, over and over, was "Joy like you." I
figured she said that to all the guys, but she was so
convincing. I really wanted to believe her.

In the morning I'd try to feed her from a big bowl of
fresh fruit that the hotel supplied. I'd say, "Joy want
banana?" And she'd always giggle, shake her head "no"
and disappear under the pillow. She could fit under the
pillow.

This time I said, "No, no, no, Joy. It's time to go,
Joy. I'm going back to New York City." And as I took
her down to the cab, she looked like a little Minnie
Mouse in high heels. And instead of getting into the
cab she pushed me into it and ran back to the hotel.
And the sliding electric glass doors opened and closed
and she stood there waving goodbye as though she lived
in the hotel and I was going home in the cab. All I could
say was, "No, no, Joy."

Tom and I gobbled some tranquilizers. In Thailand you
can buy valium right over the counter like candy. We
gobbled some valium and called our driver for the last
trip to the plane. And on that plane I was spoiled for
the last time. We got to ride in business class, high up
in those big chairs at the top of the spiral staircase.
High up above the sound of the engines. It was like

flying in a big, silent, magic motel, an airborne Holiday Inn. We pulled down our sleep masks and all I remembered was Karachi by night, a three-dollar cup of coffee in the Frankfurt airport, trying to buy a bottle of Russian vodka at Heathrow. (The lady was trying to sell me Smirnoff's and I said, "Listen lady, this is made in New Jersey." She said, "No, it's Russian. It's real Russian vodka.")

"At last, America! New York City!" And then, "Oh, my God, are we ugly!" I wasn't ready for it. New York City was bad enough but Krummville was worse. And I had had this idea that as soon as I got back I would catch up on everything—I would be a changed man. I'd adopt a Cambodian family, I'd have my teeth taken care of, pay my taxes, clean my loft—try to put it at perfect white, right angles—wash the windows, get out all the old sweaters I never wear and take them to the Cambodian refugees in Far Rockaway. I'd heard that the Cambodians march from Far Rockaway to Chinatown on the Beltway every day to buy rice because they are so confused by the subway system that they prefer walking. I saw myself as their new brother, hiking and chanting along at their sides. They'd be wearing all the old mothball-reeking V-neck sweaters that Gram Gray made for me so many years ago, that now lie at the bottom of that black trunk. At last I would do something for them. At last I'd be of service.

But instead I ended up in Krummville with Renée and it was horrid. Horrid because I didn't want to be there and I saw all the hardwoods as palm trees. At night I dreamed of taking the magic mushrooms and scuba diving with Ivan on a perfect enchanted isle somewhere in the Indian Ocean. I treated Renée like a Thai whore and I refused to go food shopping and I didn't want to cook and I was a wha-wha-wha little two-year-old. Just wha-wha-wha all over the place.

And Renée said, "Spald, calm down. Get it together. You're going to lose it. Remember how you came back to get a Hollywood agent, how you came back to make contacts and try to land another feature film? Well, we're not making any contacts here in Krummville, so I think we should go down to Bridgehampton to visit Sis and Tom. They've been nice enough to extend an invitation and you could swim in your ocean and make some contacts as well. I mean, really, I'm beginning to feel like poor white trash up here."

So we went to Bridgehampton. I had never been to the Hamptons in summer, but it was not all that unfamiliar. When I got there I recognized it from all the Michelob ads I'd seen on TV. There was this big, beautiful white house on a quarter-acre of green lawn. It was one of those beautiful turn-of-the-century houses that used to have a family in it back in the days of families, and now it was filled with beautiful couples all on the verge of breaking up, and lonely singles who had just broken up and didn't feel ready to re-commit just yet. They were all playing volleyball on the front lawn and toking up in between games, and I couldn't believe the ball just didn't turn into a seagull and swoop out over the horizon.

Next to the volleyball net was a convenient red cooler filled with Michelob, Lowenbrau, Diet Pepsi, Tab and

7-Up. And I was in charge of the bluefish—I was sure I knew about bluefish: how to buy it, how to cook it. But I wasn't in sync with the guy in charge of the coals. He had let those Briquets burn too long, so I was spraying more napalm on the coals to try and get a flame, and at the same time I made the mistake of toking off of a very strong joint and suddenly everything went prehistoric. The next thing I remember is that a group of us were all sitting around this formal table with a big white linen tablecloth and a candelabra in the center, and someone was saying, "Would you please pass the bluefish sushi?"

But I wasn't hungry. I was looking down at my hand, which was in the middle of a white plate, and it was peeling, looking like a piece of chicken with the tan peeling off like some sort of time-lapse situation in Walt Disney's *Painted Desert*. And I said, "No, thank you. I've got all I can eat right here."

And—Ahruuuuuuuuuuuuuh!—I went down on my hand, and the next thing I knew my head was in Renée's lap and I was saying, "Ahhhhhh, my God! Something awful has happened! I'm supposed to be in *Thailand*! Nothing is ever going to go right in my life again! I've ruined it!"

I fled from the table with my hand across my forehead like I had a bad case of Dostoyevskian brain fever, like Konstantin Gavrilovich in *The Seagull*. I ran out onto the porch where I threw myself into the hammock as, in the background, I heard the people at the table talking about "the gasoline-flavored bluefish sushi."

Renée rushed out to comfort me and I said, "Renée, Renée, it was a mission, a mission! I was on a mission. I'm not supposed to be back here. It wasn't just about making a film. I was about to have something revealed to me on that beach. I was supposed to be in Hanoi, I was supposed to be in Thailand. It was a mission. God wanted to speak to me through those magic mushrooms. I was on the verge of overcoming my fears, on the verge of making friends with Vietnam. It was a *mission*."

And I looked up from the hammock to see Tom Bird, this mighty Vietnam veteran, standing over me saying in a deep strong voice, "*SPALDING! BE HERE NOW!*"

And I flew back in the hammock, my face turning into a ninety-year-old man's face with a dry, twisted mouth and no teeth, and it felt like my face was falling off and the face cried, "Tom, Tom, what are you guilty about? Why couldn't you go to Paradise Beach and take the mushrooms? I know you're guilty because you killed people. You killed the Vietnamese. But why am I guilty? Why? Why?"

And Tom bellowed again, "*SPALDING! BE HERE NOW!* Do you think I want to be here?"

And suddenly I realized that this strong, silent man was also suffering. He just knew how to shut up about it.

Okay, get it together, Spalding, get it together. The next day, a little shaky and hung over, I met a couple that had just come in from sailing off Block Island. I thought, my God, that's my territory. They were sailing my seas. I was born in Rhode Island with a silver spoon in my mouth. I was born with the name Spalding Gray. Why didn't I have a big boat? What was I doing living up in Krummville at forty-two years old, when *Esquire* says I should be making my age in money?

And I came to the shocking realization that it was now too late to become a banker, a doctor, a lawyer or a psychiatrist. It was too late. But I could go to Hollywood and *play* one, and make twice as much. So I thought, "Time to get it together. Time to make some decisions," and in order to strengthen my decision-making muscles, I went to Barnes & Noble and bought a hypnotist's cassette, "How to Make Decisions—Success Series Unlimited."

Every night Renée and I would listen on the stereo earphones, and the voice would hypnotize us and put us right out. And in the morning we were supposed to drink a large glass of water to wash all the subliminal suggestions down into the subconscious. It seemed to work. I was indeed feeling more decisive.

Just around that time, I was asked to interview people under the Brooklyn Bridge, as a performance piece to commemorate the Bridge Centennial. I was to try to get them to tell personal stories about the Bridge, under the Bridge. Well, not exactly a great career choice, but at least it was a sane, simple way back into show business. And then, because of these interviews and my role in *The Killing Fields*, I was asked to come in and be interviewed by Hope Newly on WMCA Talk Radio, on a show called "For Singles Only."

Hope called me and said that she remembered me from college and would love to see me again. I couldn't quite place her but I looked forward to the interview. I was beginning to feel that I was getting back on my feet.

When I went to the Hope Newly Show, the first thing I heard was Hope interviewing a woman about her new "consciousness-raising" group for older women who

are in love with younger men. The next person who
came on was a woman discussing a cure for baldness—
and I perked up. She was saying that we don't inherit
baldness, we inherit the tendency toward oil in the
pores. And for $2,000 (money back guaranteed), you
can get a special shampoo to remove that oil, because
what's under that oil are these fully-grown hairs, like
little pig's tails, like little pubies. They're all scrunched
up in there, fully grown just waiting to pop out. And
as soon as you wash out that oil, up they pop like cork
screws. You've seen them on balding men, all combed
across the bald spot like wavy fields of Shredded Wheat.
Those are the new hairs.

Then it was my turn to come on. Hope said, "Hi,
everyone out there. This is Hope Newly, 'For Singles
Only.' And I want everyone out there to hug yourself
and say, 'Hi, me. I'm happy to be single.' All right? I
want you to welcome Spalding Gray, star of stage, screen
and television."

I don't know where she got my resume but she said,
"Spalding, I will never forget the first day that we met,
in Boston."

"Uuuum . . ."

Now this is why I don't have a house in the Hamptons, I'm convinced now. I don't know how to play
along and make myself up as I go. I said, "You're going
to have to refresh my memory, Hope. I don't remember.
I've never seen you before in my life, I swear!"

Well, she let that go and we started talking about the
film, and I could tell by the way she was reacting to
me that talking about *The Killing Fields* was like talking about cancer before there's a cure. And I figured
that her audience felt the same way, so we shifted the

subject. She said, "Well, why don't you tell our audience something about the difference between television acting and film acting. No, better still, why don't you tell them what films they may have seen you in besides *The Killing Fields*. We'll take it from there."

I took a pause and thought, well, here I go, time for fiction. Time to make myself up.

"Well, I don't know if they've seen my latest, *Leftover Life to Kill*. It's the story of the demise of Dylan Thomas, and his wife's struggle to go on after his death. I play a lesser American poet who comes to her Welsh boathouse to console her. Your audience probably hasn't seen it—it's a cult film that plays in Welsh theatres at midnight. Then there's, oh, *Time of the Assassins*. We did that in southern France and it's about Rimbaud—what a fascinating guy, what a scallywag! Do you know he gave up writing poetry at nineteen to become a gunrunner? I play a lesser American poet who visits him on his deathbed. Strange man. He had all his money hidden in his hernia truss. That one hasn't been released yet, but it's due to come out this fall."

"Well, we look forward to it. Yes."

Then I went out on a limb a little further and said, "Oh, I played a romantic lead in a ski film. I was a ski instructor in *Canadian Sunset*."

"Really?" Hope said. "How wonderful. Where was it filmed?"

Suddenly I drew a blank on all the cities in Canada . . . and then Toronto came to mind, so I just said, "Toronto."

And Hope just went and pushed me right off the limb by saying, "Toronto? I didn't know there was any skiing up there. I thought that it was all flat country."

"Oh, yes, it's very flat. Really. Actually, the film built a mountain. Fascinating to watch that. The building of the mountain was a whole film in itself and they made a separate documentary about the building of the mountain called *Too Steep to Fall*. But basically, that's the difference between film acting and TV acting. In TV, they go to the mountain and in film, they bring the mountain to them."

Now everything was going fine. I was making myself up. I've seen people make themselves up in an afternoon, become instant holy men, just make themselves up. I saw Richard Schechner do it in Central Park. It was on a lovely May day, back in the days when the Hare Krishnas used to chant from the Bowery up to Central Park, and they'd be so high by the time they reached the park that they'd look as if they were floating six inches off the pavement. They'd all come floating down the steps of Bethesda Fountain and a crowd of about two hundred people would gather around. Well, on one beautiful May Sunday, this spectacle stirred Richard's competitive juices and he took off all his clothes except for his Jockey underwear and asked me to hold them for him while he took out his Indian prayer rug, laid it by the fountain and stood on his head. This outrageous new spectacle immediately drew the crowds away from the Hares to him. I got a little panicked. It looked very much like a *Suddenly Last Summer* situation. All I could see were the soles of Richard's feet sticking up through the crowd, and I could see some of the people dropping little chunks of Italian Ices down through the holes in his underwear.

After about twenty minutes of this, Richard came down and ran over to me and said, "Quickly, give me my clothes. Let's get out of here." And as he was getting dressed I looked over to see that he had about twenty-five new converts ready to follow him anywhere. Some of them were asking, "When will you return?" As Richard answered over his shoulder, "I shall return," others asked, "Where are you going?" And Richard said, "I am walking east."

I think they would have followed him right into the East River without a doubt in their heads.

Now, to some extent, Sri Rama Krishna also made himself up. He was an actor of sorts. He was the last great Indian saint who didn't have twenty-nine Rolls Royces—the last great *poor* Indian guru.

Sri Rama Krishna went through a number of dynamic character transformations in which he became the people he worshipped. Although he was a Hindu, he was in no way hung up on one religion. He embraced them all. When he worshipped Christ, he became Christ; when he worshipped Buddha, he became him. He even performed his tantric practices with a woman and when he worshipped Mother Kali he *became* a woman and people in the Kali temple would mistake him for one. He had no sense of self. He was an actor, a conduit, a man without an identity. And because he lived in India, he didn't have to go to a psychiatrist. He was seen as a holy man and not as a psychotic. At last, a naked sadhu ran out of the jungle, stuck a sharp stone between Sri Rama's eyes and he saw Nothing.

Now, who are the holy people in the West? Actors and actresses. They are the only people who can say they don't know who they are and not be put away in an insane asylum for it. Peter Sellers, the actor, was not unlike Sri Rama Krishna to the extent that he made himself up and acted as a conduit through which he allowed many voices to pass. Sellers insisted that he never knew who he was. In the West that was a problem, so he had to go to a psychiatrist, but in my mind, he was a kind of holy man. And in our utilitarian, materialistic world, where is Mecca for these holy people of the West? It's the furthest west they can go without going east. It's Hollywood. And where does their immortality have its being? On film. The image set forever in celluloid. And who is God? The camera. The ever-present, omniscient third eye. And what is the Holy Eucharist? Money!

So I said, "I'm going!" And I put on the magic John Malkovich suit, the brown one, I took my Thai *bhat* and converted it into $600, got a ticket on TWA and headed out to Hollywood to select an agent.

After the plane took off without crashing, I was opening one of those fucking little salad dressing packets and—"Oh, *shit*! Oh, Lord, why does this always happen the one time I put a suit on? Chewing gum flies to me on the subway and sticks. Salad dressing eats through my new pants."

This traveling salesman next to me said, "Don't worry about it, take it right in to the cleaners as soon as you get there. Hope it's colorfast. Where'd you have it made?"

"Bangkok."

"Oh. Well I don't know about that. You never know how those guys will put something together."

So as soon as I arrived in Venice I took my suit to the cleaners and rushed right down to see the boardwalk. I was so excited to be in a large city that was so close to a major ocean—I couldn't wait to see and breathe that ocean. I couldn't wait to see and walk on that boardwalk I'd heard so much about. I thought, the agent can wait for a day. I'm going to see that Pacific Ocean.

When I got down to the boardwalk I was a little disappointed to find that there were no boards. It turned out to be an asphalt walk. But still, I was excited to be by the ocean, and as I was walking along that asphalt boardwalk with a bounce, breathing deep, an unmarked car pulled up behind me and two unmarked guys jumped out. Holding chrome-plated forty-fives with both hands, they braced themselves on the top of the open car doors and almost blew away two winos. I thought I was in a movie or at least on *Hill Street Blues*, and I ducked behind a pizza counter. I watched these two unmarked men run up and press the barrels of their guns right to the winos' heads, handcuff their arms behind them, knee them in the back and then throw them into the unmarked car. I thought, Lordy, Lordy, this is dangerous territory. I better go get my magic John Malkovich suit on. But the suit wasn't ready yet, and soon cocktail hour rolled around.

I decided to ride out on my borrowed ten-speed bike in search of beer. I found a little beer store on a side road and went in and bought a king-size can of Rainier

Ale, and I just couldn't wait to get home—I opened it right outside the store. I was brown-bagging and chug-a-lugging just like I would in New York, when this L.A.P.D. cruiser came full speed down the little side-street and did a U-turn. And something about the way the car turned made me think that maybe they were after me. Like they had beer radar. And I wondered, can it be that they would take time out of their busy schedule to bust me for drinking one king-size can of Rainier Ale?

Not wanting to take any chances, I chucked it into a cardboard box beside me which was filled with empty beer cans. The police pulled up and shined the spotlight attached to the side of their car right on that box, and the two of them got out of the car and went over and pulled out the very can from which I'd been drinking. Somehow they were able to pick that can out from all the others. And they pushed me up against the wall of the beer store and made me put my hands over my head while they searched me with a club.

"What's your name? Where's your I.D.?"

"I don't have my wallet. I left it back at the house where I'm staying—and my name is Spalding Gray."

"Oh, yeah? What do they call you?"

"They call me Spalding Gray. I swear it."

And one of the cops said, "Okay, get in the car," while the other one put my bike in the trunk. And just as I was getting into the cruiser the cop who was handling my bike demanded to search me.

"Okay, I know my partner's searched you but we like to do double searches around here just to make sure."

So I got searched again and then they put me in the back of the cruiser and said, "What's the address of the house you're staying at?" And for a moment I blanked out. Then I remembered six days in a Las Vegas jail in 1977 for refusing to give my name to an officer when first asked, and I remembered 9227 Boccaccio. It just came to me like that—and I thought, oh my God, I'm getting good. I'm getting healthier. I'm on my way to success.

They drove me there. It was a very short trip and when we got there one cop stayed in the car to guard me while the other went into 9227 Boccaccio to find out if anyone knew one Spalding Gray. And luckily, someone there knew me that day and the cop came right back out and said, "Okay, get your bike out of the trunk and consider yourself lucky for getting a free ride home."

I would rather have ridden my bike home, I thought, but I didn't tell them that. What I did say was, "Look, I don't want to sound ungrateful or testy, but I just flew in from New York City and people brown-bag all the time in New York, so I didn't know."

The cop replied in a very stern voice, like a voice I remembered from boarding school, "I think if you check your New York City laws you'll find that it's against the law to drink in the streets. We just happen to enforce our laws here in L.A."

Right to bed! The next day I got up bright and early, feeling like a new man, and I went and got my suit out of the cleaners and got my friends to drive me to Ugly Duckling Car Rental, which was the cheapest I could find. I rented an Ugly Duckling Toyota. The only problem with the car that I could see was that the seat was broken so that it was at the angle of a lounge chair, and I could barely see over the windshield.

By that time I had boiled it all down to two agencies. If both were interested I would have to make the choice between them. One was Writers and Artists and the other was Smith Freedman Associates. First, I visited Writers and Artists and they were very nice—I think they wanted to sign me. The only problem, as I saw it, was that they were not "other" enough. They were too much like My People. They were very WASPy and I could see them all wearing topsiders and vacationing on Martha's Vineyard. Also, I wasn't sure if it would be such a good idea to be represented under the title "Writers and Artists" in this day and age if, in fact, I wanted to make enough money to buy a house in the Hamptons.

So I decided to drive over and see Susan Smith at Smith Freedman Associates, and if she wanted to sign me I'd do it. As soon as I walked into her office she said, "We want you. We want to sign you right now."

Well, I was kind of sober about all this because it was all so smiley, all going so fast. I responded in my very serious and rather ponderous East Coast way, "Well, that's nice, isn't it? Now let me think about it."

And Susan said, "Would you have smiled if we said we didn't want you?" Then she said, "Let's go, we don't have time for this. You've got one day left out here and we want to send you out to all the casting agents in town just to say, 'Hi. I'm a new face in town and I'm with Smith Freedman.' "

They gave me a map of all the studios and I headed out to the first stop, Warner Brothers, to audition for *The Karate Kid*. They had me read for the role of the tough guy, the kind of karate killer who teaches all the neighborhood kids his aggressive, evil ways. Well, you can imagine how that went.

The next stop was *Hill Street Blues*, which went a little better. Gerri Windsor, the casting director, was very nice and she told me that if I moved out there she could almost guarantee me some work on the show. I asked her how she could say that when she hadn't even auditioned me, and she said, "New faces. We're always looking for new faces and you're a new face. With a good agent. So I think we're pretty safe in saying that if you move out here we can get you work—but you have to live out here because we really can't afford to fly you out."

So I left *Hill Street* and continued to follow my little map to ABC, NBC and CBS. All was going fine, but by noon I understood why all actors out there have air-conditioned cars. My Ugly Duckling wasn't air-conditioned and I was beginning to leak through my shirt. Also, that hot, dry air was turning my hair into an insane frizzball. I was coming unglued. And by the time I reached Twentieth Century-Fox I looked like a madman.

I parked the Ugly Duckling, being careful not to park it within eye-view of the casting director's office because I'd heard that they look out to see what you're driving, and the Ugly Duckling was not looking good in comparison to the other cars in that lot. I went into the office and was happy and surprised to find that the receptionist recognized me from my monologues—and she was excited to see me.

"Oh, Spalding Gray, what are you doing here looking for work? You should be working all the time. You could play a lawyer, you could play a doctor, you could play a psychiatrist . . ."

I went inside the casting director's office and quickly realized that she had no idea who I was, beyond being a "new face." There was something both comforting and discomforting about being there. The comforting part was the physical office itself, the fantastic white couch and the way in which it received me as I sank in and slowly gave up all thoughts of ever moving again. Also, the clean view out the window of lush palms and pines, coupled with the secure feeling of being in that oh-so-clean, solid room. And most of all, the way the corners of the ceiling and walls came together at perfect, solid, white, right angles. But the discomforting part of the experience came when she told me that she just called me in to see me, "have a look," I think she meant. But she said, "We've heard all about you and now we'd like to see you."

And we made small talk while she looked and I could feel my imperfect jawline sagging, my face puffing and my bald spot shining. I could see all those things and I suddenly and clearly realized what it feels like to be a woman scrutinized by a man. I've hardly ever had that feeling before. Only in Morocco.

But that big, soft couch had made me feel secure, and I found that I had made it on time, without getting lost or arrested, to all my interviews and I felt a kind of Triumph of the Will as I sped along the freeways in my little Ugly Duckling.

The only problem was that the front seat had fallen all the way back and was now resting on the back seat. I was using this as a positive experience by holding myself erect by the wheel and giving my stomach muscles a good isometric workout. It was wonderful to be out on the open freeway again and feeling that I had willed it all, and also feeling, isn't it funny that after you've willed something you wonder why you wanted to will it in the first place? But it felt good anyway.

Think of it, I considered, way back on the beaches of Thailand I wanted an agent and now I've got one. I've willed it and I got it and isn't that what everyone out here wants?

An agent. Even my friends the Cambodian refugees from Long Beach wanted to know how they could get an agent. They had suddenly found that they were in a very good feature film and were sure that the next logical step in the progression was to get a Hollywood agent. When I went to visit them they asked me if I could help them get one. An agent. An agent. "Can you help us get an agent?" I wanted to help but I couldn't imagine where Cambodians would find steady work in the Industry. Then a very perverse idea occurred to me. Norman Lear had just produced a sitcom called *A.K.A. Pablo* that had given a lot of Chicanos steady work. Perhaps the new sitcom of the eighties could be *A.K.A. Pol Pot*—which would give all my Cambodian friends a lot of work.

It wasn't all that far-fetched. I got the idea from a very poignant film I had seen at the Margaret Mead Festival a few years earlier. The film was about the relocation of the Laotian Hmong tribes. After the CIA lost the war in Laos all the Hmongs had to get out fast because they sided with "the American military effort in Laos." The film was about their relocation from Thai refugee camps to immigrant condos in Washington State.

They all arrived at these furnitureless condominiums that had wall-to-wall shag carpeting as long as your fingers. I guess they saw the shag as a kind of organic growth so they began by washing it down with a garden hose and then sweeping the water into a heating duct, thinking it was a drain. After that they tried to cook chicken breasts in the toaster. It was all very sad and very funny at the same time.

The supermarket confused them totally. Thinking it was a bar of soap, they bought a big, yellow block of Velveeta cheese. This is how I picture the opening shot of the sitcom: a Cambodian singing "Do You Want to Funk?" in the shower as he washes under his arms with a large yellow block of Velveeta, which is breaking into chunks from the hot water and washing down the drain in yellow streams.

So I had gotten an agent by willing it and I was home-free on the freeway, and didn't it feel oh-so-good to put the pedal to the metal and spin. Turn up the radio and blast. And, yes, I could do it, we could do it. Renée and I could move out here and have a little house in a canyon. A little bungalow which all came together in solid, clean, white, right angles. We could do it. I could get some work on *Hill Street*, *St. Elsewhere* or *Knots Landing* and we could do it.

I would come home exhausted after a day's work at the studio and instead of having cocktail hour, I'd go jogging around the reservoir while Renée arranged sun-dried tomatoes and smoked mozzarella and tossed a big bowl of sprouts and leafy greens. We could do it. And I'd come in all sinewy and tired, just wanting to eat

and rest and be with, and sleep with, my little Renée.
My little sweetie. And soon the beautiful children would
come along and there'd be fun with them on weekends
out in the high desert, or downwind, surfing off Venice.
And we'd make it. The kids would grow up and we'd
have enough money to send them to good schools. Renée
and I would grow old together and we'd make it. We'd
make it through.

Then the freeway would grind down into an impossible
gridlock situation and clog with smog. And the Ugly
Duckling would come almost to a dead stop, and the
image of MX missiles flying low over pine trees would
flash in my mind. I needed to get back. I had to get
back to the East Coast to save the world and stop the
war.

And wasn't life about service? Didn't I have enough
pleasure in my life and wasn't it now time to help ease
the pain of others? And the Bodhisatva's vow came to
me: If all people can't reside in a state of pleasure in
Southern California, then no one can until all can. And
I could see the State of California collapsing, not from
earthquakes, but from the weight of the world as all
the wretched of the earth clamored toward the sun that
broke through bare lemon trees and devoured fruit
bushes. How could I think of my pleasure when the
world still suffered so? How? How? How? Oh, the shame
of it!

I needed to get back to give my old sweaters away
to the Cambodian refugees in Far Rockaway. And the
death image of Jean Donovan—chopped to death in El
Salvador—came to me. And the *Cocktail Party* voice

of Celia Coplestone from her anthill crucifixion played in my ears:

> But first I must tell
>   you
> That I should really LIKE to think there's something
>   wrong with me—
> Because, if there isn't then there's something wrong,
> Or at least, very different from what it seemed to
>   be,
> With the world itself—and that's much more
>   frightening!
> That would be terrible. So I'd rather believe
> There is something wrong with me, that could be
>   put right.

And I thought, I've got to get back where it all counts. I've got to get back.

Then the traffic would pick up and everything would feel clear, as the not-so-long-dead voice of Alan Watts floated up from his Sausalito houseboat saying, "Relax, Spalding, relax. Enjoy. You're in California now. What is there to feel guilty about? Relax. Enjoy. Life's a party. So what if you came in at the end of it? Relax. Enjoy."

I made it back to Venice and had a couple of good-sized shots of tequila and went to bed. And I had this dream.

I was babysitting for a boy in a cabin in the woods. There was this huge fireplace, and the boy kept playing a game with me where he would run into the fireplace and get partially consumed by the flames and then run out—just before he was completely consumed—and reconstitute himself. I was very nervous. I was watching him out of the corner of my eye and all of a sudden he ran in and I saw that he was completely in flames. There was no torso left and the flames were in the shape of legs, flame-legs. And I grabbed the fire-poker to try to pull him out and . . . nothing. It just went right through the flames; there was no substance. And the flames burned down and left this pile of gray ash on the hearth.

I turned to see, in the corner of the cabin, a straw boy, an effigy of the real boy. And I took the gray ash in my hands and went over and blew it into the straw boy's side. Slowly, the effigy came alive. And his face had this great, ear-to-ear, joyous, all-knowing, friendly smile as he shook his head. And I realized that he hadn't wanted to come back, that he had chosen to be consumed by the flames—and then the spirit went out of the straw boy and I was left holding this empty, straw effigy in my arms. I thought, how am I ever going to tell this story to his mother? No one will believe me. And I went searching for someone to tell the story to. I found that I was wandering through the streets of Hollywood.

The first person I came across was Ron Vawter, an actor friend from a theatre company called The Wooster Group, and I told Ron the story. He said, "You should have called the police right away. You need a witness with authority. There's no way you're going to prove that this happened and there's no way you can reenact it."

I left Ron and continued my search for the straw boy's mother, and came upon Elizabeth LeCompte, the director of The Wooster Group. She was sitting, drinking orangeade with the boy's mother by a Hollywood pool.

I started to tell them the story but I couldn't articulate it and instead of telling the Straw Boy Story, in a very loud, theatrical voice I said, "THE REASON I'M UP-SET IS THAT I WAS JUST IN A NEW PECKINPAH MOVIE OF CHEKHOV'S SEAGULL . . ."

And I had played the role of Konstantin Gavrilovich, the writer who shoots himself in the head at the end of the play . . .

"AND WHAT I'M UPSET ABOUT—IS THAT I SAW THE FILM, I LIKED IT, BUT I CAN'T REMEMBER DOING IT. I can't remember acting in it. All I saw was an image with no memory attached."

And I knew all the time I was telling this story that it was a cover for the real story, the Straw Boy Story, which, for some reason, I found impossible to tell.

Afterword

▽   ▽   ▽   ▽   ▽   ▽

James Leverett

This is a recording. Spalding Gray's *Swimming to Cambodia*, that is. It is a record as history is a record. Dare I say that it is a new form as well, or really an old one reasserting itself in a new way? Call it an "epic monologue," remembering what "epic" has meant during the several millenia of its history: a text performed first, written down later; a vessel for great themes expressed through mighty events extending past earthbound reality up into the splendor of paradise and down into the devastation of hell; a canvas of life forever on the move between the individual and universal, and always beset by the irony of mortality; a confluence of history and myth.

An over-inflated order for a couple of hours on the stage, to be sure—especially hours spent with someone so entertaining and downright hilarious as Gray. But the two parts of *Swimming to Cambodia* are such rich, deep reflections on the world as we are obliged to live in it right now, and so clearly culminations of work their author has been creating for several years, that they invite hyperbole.

Gray's life as a performer is an important part of the history of American avant-garde theatre over the past generation. He was active in the 1960s and 1970s with Richard Schechner and the Performance Group, continuing with that theatre after Schechner's departure and its transformation into the present Wooster Group, one of the most exciting, innovative experimental ensembles operating anywhere today. It was from parts of Gray's personal history, particularly the events surrounding the suicide of his mother, that director Elizabeth LeCompte fashioned the *Rhode Island Trilogy*, the Wooster Group's first work and its first typically controversial artistic success.

Adjacent to those complex, ensemble performances of his past, Gray developed his own monologues which have inevitably become ongoing explorations of his present. First, there was *Sex and Death to the Age 14* (childhood to puberty), then *Booze, Cars and College Girls* (young manhood), A *Personal History of the American Theatre* (his early career as an actor), *India and After* (the times and, to a degree, the life of the Performance Group), right up to *Interviewing the Audience* (which is just that).

When he first sat down behind a modest wooden table, took an almost calibrated sip from a glass of water and began to read from his journals about memories of early erections and the death of pets, Gray surely did not realize that his experiment would become the focal point of a vast range of performance art which would dominate New York's Soho and other bastions of the artistic vanguard during the 1970s. He became a major influence in that work, praised as an original by some, damned as a perpetrator of the "me-decade" by others. (After all! A guy sitting at a table just talking about himself!)

It would be incorrect to think that these early monologues, eight in all, could be written down and served up end-to-end to total a neat autobiography. All are impressionistic; all weave back and forth in time and place to form tapestries of intertwining themes and imagery which only occasionally reveal a strand of sequential narrative. Some are experimental in the extreme: In *India and After*, for example (the first monologue that was not strictly "mono"), a partner chooses words from an unabridged dictionary to which Gray responds with free associations having to do with his trips to India and across the United States during the early 1970s.

Likewise, it would be false to consider these pieces to be the narcissistic exercises of an actor's overgrown ego, unconcerned with such irrelevant externals as politics, history and society. *Sex and Death* begins and ends with two cataclysmic punctuations: the A-bomb dropped at Hiroshima, the H-bomb at Enewetak. What Gray conveys in between, albeit in the subtlest and most indirect way, is the coming of age in this country after World War II. All of the monologues have had such an added, often hidden, dimension. If you stare at any one of them long enough, you find that what has happened to Gray reflects in a startlingly illuminating way what has happened to the world, or at least a significant section of it, you and I certainly included.

But such allegorical relationships are never explicit, or even apparently deliberate. Each new work is a new development of the Gray persona, which could be characterized as an incorrigible witness, mirror or, well, sponge. And as the material moves through his childhood past into his adult here-and-now, the autobiographical "I" more and more shares the stage with the bystander "he." It has gradually become Gray's chosen lot simultaneously to live his life and to play the role of Spalding Gray living his life, *and* to observe said Gray living his life in order to report on it in the next monologue. Perhaps this hall of mirrors, this endless playoff between performance and reality, has always been the situation of the artist. It is certainly the quintessential perspective of the actor, though seldom dramatized so blatantly. But has it ever been more plainly the predicament of everyone else in this media-ridden age of instant replay? Conditioned by McLuhan and Warhol, Johnny Carson and Phil Donahue, we are all to an extent the subject of our own self-writing life story, our shoot-as-you-go movie. The possibility of celebrity for everyone seems to grow with each newscast.

So Spalding Gray got a minor role in *The Killing Fields*, a movie about the recent—one could say continuing—history of Cambodia. It was shot in Thailand, next door to where it originally happened (continues to happen), and in Hollywood, where everything pretends (or aspires) to happen. And he made a monologue about Cambodia, Thailand, Hollywood—and Spalding Gray.

As remarkable as they all are, the previous monologues now seem like test flights for the virtuosic swoops and dives of the Cambodia pieces. In them, those poles by which what we call reality are measured tumble over one another like dice in a crap shoot: fiction over history, madness over sanity, microcosm over macrocosm, dream over reality. A sailor likes blue-flake cocaine, kinky threesomes and the nuclear detonator to which he is handcuffed; a President watches George C. Scott in *Patton* and tells a gathering of war protesters how travel improves the mind; a corporate vice president reads *An Actor Prepares*. A small country of exquisite people—an innocent paradise—transforms itself into hell-on-earth, stirred to genocidal frenzy by Mao, Rousseau and B-52s. But, are those slaughtered peasants or day-players cosmetized with stage blood and chicken giblets? Are those burning villages or burning tires set out by the special-effects crew? Is this history or just another take? Through this landscape in which everything threatens to become something else, Gray wanders, the essential white-bread WASP, skirting the shore to avoid the sharks, looking for an agent, afraid he will miss the fun, staying too long at the party, asking simple questions, getting terrifying answers, searching for the Perfect Moment.

This is a recording. For the first time, Gray's odyssey has been taken down. What in his monologues has always seemed to be writing, hovering just above the little table from which he performs, is now written. We lose the wry, desultory, curious living presence of a master storyteller. But we gain the opportunity to make our own replays again and again, and to take the measure of an achievement that seems to grow with each encounter—perhaps even to epic proportions.